D1250008

IDEAS,
IDEALS, AND
AMERICAN DIPLOMACY

IDEAS, IDEALS, AND AMERICAN DIPLOMACY:

A HISTORY OF THEIR GROWTH AND INTERACTION

ARTHUR A. EKIRCH, JR.
STATE UNIVERSITY OF NEW YORK AT ALBANY

APPLETON-CENTURY-CROFTS
NEW YORK
DIVISION OF MEREDITH PUBLISHING COMPANY

TO

WILLIAM L. NEUMANN

Prefatory Note

The present work which, of necessity, rests on the research and writings of a number of scholars is an effort to summarize some of the major themes that have guided the historic course of American diplomacy. It is offered both as an aid to college students and as a survey for the interested general public which, in a democracy, must ever be the final arbiter of the mainstream of national thought and action with respect to foreign affairs.

Source materials and quotations are identified in the footnotes, while the Selected References, placed at the close of each chapter, list the more important secondary books. The special emphasis, however, is on those volumes which treat foreign policy in terms of its ideological content. As a result, some of the more familiar, traditional treatises are not always included. Of the many excellent general surveys and texts, I found particularly useful Thomas A. Bailey's *A Diplomatic History of the American People* (Appleton-Century-Crofts) and two anthologies, *Ideas and Diplomacy* (Oxford University Press) by Norman A. Graebner and *The Shaping of American Diplomacy* (Rand McNally and Co.) by William Appleman Williams.

I am deeply grateful to Professor Thomas A. Bailey of Stanford University and Professor William L. Neumann of Goucher College for their careful reading of the manuscript. I also wish to thank Mrs. Naomi Wood for typing the final draft. The dedication to Professor Neumann is a token of my appreciation for his continuing friendly interest and help in my research and writing.

Contents

Foreword

The determination of American foreign policy has always been an interesting and important part of our national history. From the time when America was a colony of the British Empire to its current position as colossus of the modern world, the United States has seldom been free of concern over foreign affairs. Since the days of the Founding Fathers, the written record of American diplomacy has comprised an often exciting and significant segment of our intellectual heritage. In no respect is this more true than in the study of the ideas traditionally associated with American foreign policy. Ideology and concrete national interests together have shaped the course of United States diplomacy, and in the interplay of ideals and interests there has been not only a powerful motivation toward some particular line of policy, but also frequently a rationalization for events and actions of the past.

For most nations throughout modern history, time-honored ideals as well as long-standing concepts of self-interest have combined to influence the conduct of foreign affairs. It has been argued, however, that ideals and morality serve only to hinder the workings of international diplomacy and to obscure the actual national interest. On the other hand, it seems true that a definition of national interest which operates exclusively on a Machiavellian plane of power politics can run the equal and opposite danger of sacrificing popular leadership and influence. Ideals which do not adequately reflect realistic national concerns, however, may serve only to bestow the accolade of a hypocritical morality upon diplomacy. Policies conceived in careful consideration of long-range national interests may, therefore, be more genuinely moral than pious diplomatic excursions in public duplicity and deception.

In modern political society it is probably a fact that national leadership can heighten foreign crises to the point where war becomes almost inevitable and public approval, at least for a time, automatic. All too often in history, we know that political leaders have sought to obviate domestic discontents by arousing the popular mind over dangers, real or pretended, from abroad. American statesmen on occasion have been wont to still public criticism by exaggerating the merits of bipartisan support for the nation's foreign policy. Such a course, however, can endanger the fundamentals of representative government and the two-party system. It may also stultify the power of public opinion, forestalling popular criticism and contributing to a general apathy in respect to foreign affairs. At the same time, it should be noted that public opinion can be corrupted, not only by official propaganda, but also by the selfish interests of private pressure groups. Thus public opinion, by the very fact of its importance for the conduct of foreign affairs in a democracy, is ever subject to the dangers of control or manipulation.

The study of foreign policy, it is clear, involves more than the restricted story of the negotiations carried on by each country's diplomatic personnel. Foreign policy, like domestic policy, has to be considered in relation to a nation's history and culture. From its establishment as a free and independent nation, through its rise to a position of primacy in the world, the development of the United States has been affected by ideas of isolationism, manifest destiny and mission, nationalism, imperialism, internationalism, peace, and democracy. In our own time, the idea of a new world order competes with the concept of a *pax Americana*. Thus today, as in the past, currents of nationalism and internationalism continue to be in conflict. And, these ideals, in their relation to American foreign policy, have seldom been fraught with as much worldwide meaning and importance as they are today.

SELECTED REFERENCES

Almond, Gabriel A. *The American People and Foreign Policy*. New York: Harcourt, Brace, 1950.
Bailey, Thomas A. *The Man in the Street: The Impact of American Public Opinion on Foreign Policy*. New York: Macmillan, 1948.

Beard, Charles A. *The Idea of National Interest: An Analytical Study in American Foreign Policy.* New York: Macmillan, 1934.

Beloff, Max. *Foreign Policy and the Democratic Process.* Baltimore: Johns Hopkins Press, 1955.

Cook, Thomas I. and Malcolm Moos. *Power Through Purpose: The Realism of Idealism As a Basis for Foreign Policy.* Baltimore: Johns Hopkins Press, 1954.

Kennan, George F. *American Diplomacy, 1900–1950.* Chicago: University of Chicago Press, 1951.

Lerche, Charles O. *Foreign Policy of the American People.* Englewood Cliffs, N.J.: Prentice-Hall, 1958.

Morgenthau, Hans J. *In Defense of National Interest: A Critical Examination of American Foreign Policy.* New York: Knopf, 1951.

Morley, Felix. *The Foreign Policy of the United States.* New York: Knopf, 1951.

Niebuhr, Reinhold. *The Irony of American History.* New York: Scribner, 1952.

Osgood, Robert E. *Ideals and Self-Interest in America's Foreign Relations.* Chicago: University of Chicago Press, 1953.

Perkins, Dexter. *The American Approach to Foreign Policy.* Cambridge, Mass.: Harvard University Press, 1952.

Williams, William A. *The Tragedy of American Diplomacy.* Cleveland: World, 1959.

I

The Isolationist Tradition

The foreign policy of the United States had its beginnings in the desire for American political freedom. Like most new nations, the United States was strongly nationalistic in its early diplomacy. Its ultimate goal, naturally enough, was the achievement of independence from Great Britain. Until full sovereignty and national security could be assured—and the latter was not certain until the conclusion of the War of 1812—the diplomacy of the United States was of necessity narrowly nationalistic in its motivation. Other matters of possible interest and importance were subordinated to this one essential goal.

Because the major European states—England, France, and Spain —had rival interests in the New World that might encroach upon American freedom, it was the policy of the Continental Congress to regard all foreign nations with considerable suspicion. Although the United States could not avoid being affected by the course of events in Europe, its statesmen readily concluded that American independence should not be jeopardized by any unnecessary or direct political involvement in European affairs.

Commercial and cultural contacts, on the other hand, were not thought to be in conflict with political separation from the Old World. Such representatives of the eighteenth-century Enlightenment in America as Benjamin Franklin and Thomas Jefferson were, after all, themselves cosmopolitan figures with strong international ties and experience. Americans, moreover, desired to expand their foreign trade. Southern planters, no less than New England merchants, were interested in world markets, and political isolationism was not taken to imply exclusion from the prospective economic benefits overseas that might flow from independence.

Isolationism as an expression of early American foreign policy

1

was therefore a means, not an end. A political separation which did not entail a complete intellectual and economic divorce from Europe, it was calculated to satisfy the demands of most American patriots. At the same time, however, isolationism was already on the way to becoming an important American ideal simply because it fitted in so well with the national interests of the young Republic.

England at the time of the first settlements in North America was already a strong national state. By the middle of the eighteenth century, the British people had emerged victorious from a series of wars against the Spanish, Dutch, and French empires. Separated from the European Continent by the English Channel, Britain strengthened its navy and protected itself from invasion. While geography thereby contributed to the sense of isolation and security of the British Isles, at the same time its insular position also encouraged the English nation to look overseas to the building of an empire.

In the United States, ideas of isolationism, nationalism, and economic expansion were all aspects of an American foreign policy which had its origins in the experience of England itself. Indeed, it has been suggested that the early American doctrine of isolation rested on British precedents. Both Benjamin Franklin and Thomas Paine applied the lesson of Britain's isolated insular position to the similar advantageous situation of the American colonies. In *Common Sense* Paine urged English isolationist arguments to justify American independence and freedom from Europe's wars and kings. Early American isolationism accordingly was both derived from England and a reaction, via the American Revolution, against England.

Although the Revolutionary movement culminated in the waging of a war for national self-determination, the American colonists until 1776 remained remarkably reluctant to separate themselves from the Mother Country. In some ways the Revolution was more a civil war within the British Empire, in which Americans fought to preserve what they regarded as their rights and liberties as Englishmen. As Cushing Strout points out, the colonists prized their English heritage, upheld British institutions, and even thought of themselves symbolically as "of purer English Blood."

The American Revolution was, in fact, less a popular revulsion against an alien tyranny than it was a tragic civil war. The colonists had challenged their oppressors by appealing to the glorious traditions of English history. Whatever revolutionary theory they had devised was borrowed from England's own John Locke, who had rationalized the settlement of 1688. To their disillusionment they ultimately found that the ideals they revered were better cherished in the New World than in the Old World that had given birth to them.[1]

Loyalty to England and the development of what has been called an Atlantic civilization in the eighteenth century had to compete, however, with an emerging spirit of Americanism among the thirteen Colonies. Improved modes of transportation and communication, a common frontier, joint warfare against the Indians, plus the rather half-hearted cooperation among the colonies in their struggles against French power in North America, all helped to break down provincial separatism and to encourage a degree of intercolonial cooperation. The rising tide of European immigration and the number of religious sects among the colonists also contributed to the growth of a new, non-English culture. Thus the English heritage was continually being modified by the impact of the American environment with its greater vitality, variety, and enormous economic potential.

Before the influence of American ways reached its climax in the Revolution, it had already fostered a widespread feeling that the long-range future of the British Empire lay with the North American Continent. As early as 1760 Benjamin Franklin told his British friend Lord Kames: "I have long been of opinion, that the *foundations of the future grandeur and stability of the British empire lie in America.* . . ." Though Franklin supported union with the Mother Country, he considered it of more advantage to Britain than to the colonies. In any case, he wrote in 1767, "America, an immense territory, favored by Nature with all the advantages of climate, soil, great navigable rivers, and lakes, etc. must become a great country, populous and mighty; and will, in a less time than is generally conceived, be able to shake off any shackles that may be imposed on her. . . ." A few years later Franklin criticized the English social system that depressed "Multitudes below the Savage State that a few may be rais'd above it," and in 1775 he noted "the extream Corrup-

<hr>

[1] Cushing Strout, *The American Image of the Old World* (New York, 1963), 12.

tion prevalent among all Orders of Men in this old rotten State. . . ."[2]

Confident of their prospective advantages, and no longer sure that the British Government was the best guardian of their security or liberties, the American colonists were willing to be persuaded to undertake the manifest risks of independence. Despite growing dissatisfaction, however, a decade of petitions and protests airing American grievances against King George and his ministers had not made clear the positive gains that might be realized by separation. It was the particular merit of Tom Paine's *Common Sense,* therefore, that it presented the first fully developed argument setting forth the advantages to be gained by breaking away from Great Britain.

Paine, who had arrived in America barely a year before the fighting at Lexington and Concord, stated a thesis that many of the American colonists were finally ready to accept. The Revolutionary movement in America had reached the stage, he pointed out, where prized English rights and liberties would be better safeguarded for Americans if they severed all political connection with the Mother Country and its monarchical institutions. "Reconciliation is *now* a fallacious dream," he wrote. "A government of our own is our natural right." Although there were those who contended that England and the colonies united might defy the rest of the world, it was not in the interest of America to be drained of inhabitants to support British arms. "Besides," Paine continued, "what have we to do with setting the world at defiance? Our plan is commerce, and that, well attended to, will secure us the peace and friendship of all Europe. . . . I challenge the warmest advocate for reconciliation to show a single advantage that this continent can reap, by being connected with Great Britain." Dependence on Britain meant involvement in European wars, while the correct policy for America was peace, friendship, and trade with all nations. "It is the true interest of America to steer clear of European contentions, which she can never do, while, by her dependence on Britain she is made the make-weight in the scale of British politics." [3]

Some months before Paine's celebrated pamphlet was published, John Adams, according to his later recollection, had already argued in the Continental Congress that the future independence of the American colonies would depend on neutrality and no entangling alliances with European nations. From the French Adams wanted "only a commercial convention" without political or military ties. In any alliance between a foreign nation and America, Adams feared, "we should be little better off than puppets, danced on the wires of the cabinets of Europe. We should be the sport of European intrigue and politics; that, therefore, in preparing treaties to be proposed to foreign powers, and in the instructions to be given to our ministers, we ought to confine ourselves strictly to a treaty of commerce; that such a treaty would be ample compensation to France for all the aid we should want from her." In any case, he felt that in regard to France "we ought not to enter into any alliance with her which should entangle us in any future wars in Europe; that we ought to lay it down, as a first principle and a maxim never to be forgotten, to maintain an entire neutrality in all future European wars. . . ." [4]

As late as 1777, Adams remained undismayed by the lack of a political and military connection with France. If the United States could enjoy the advantages of free trade with Europe, he was willing for America to incur the risks of fighting Britain alone. To such isolationist views the American Revolution was the most powerful reinforcement. In the words of Dexter Perkins: "The Revolution itself was an act of isolation, a cutting of the ties with the Old World, the deed of a society which felt itself different from those which existed on the other side of the Atlantic, and which was, indeed, unique in its composition and its aspirations." [5]

Like John Adams, many of his fellow members in the Continental Congress would have preferred to have confined French help

3 *Writings of Thomas Paine*, M. D. Conway, ed. (New York, 1906–1908), I, 91, 99, 88–89.

4 *Works of John Adams*, C. F. Adams, ed. (Boston, 1850–1856), II, 488–489, 505–506.

5 Dexter Perkins, *The American Approach to Foreign Policy* (Cambridge, Mass., 1952), 10.

in the Revolution to economic aid and a commercial treaty. Thus the Continental Congress at the first opportunity dispatched commercial agents abroad in the hope of securing favorable trade relations. The dire military situation in 1776 and 1777, threatening the whole cause of American independence, persuaded the United States to go further, however, and ratify the full French Treaty of Alliance which Benjamin Franklin was able to negotiate after the battle of Saratoga. By the terms of the treaty the United States was committed to support French objectives in any war which might, and indeed was likely to, follow between England and France. Although it definitely entangled America in the affairs of Europe, from an American standpoint the treaty's most important provision was its statement that "The essential and direct End of the present defensive alliance is to maintain effectually the liberty, Sovereignty and independence absolute and unlimited, of the said united States, as well in Matters of Gouvernement as of commerce." [6]

Even before the Revolution was concluded and independence achieved—in large part as a result of French military and economic aid—the Treaty of Alliance had already become an encumbrance to the United States, a diplomatic commitment to be ended as soon as possible. Rising American nationalism, plus apprehensions over possible French and Spanish territorial ambitions in the New World, aroused American jealousies. In Puritan New England there were misgivings about association with a Catholic king and country. In the Continental Congress a Connecticut delegate questioned whether it would not have been better to have tried to fight on without the alliance, and Henry Laurens of South Carolina also expressed his doubts about "our delicate connection with France." [7] Unsuccessful American-French military operations up until the final victory at Yorktown, and the complications resulting from France's alliance with Spain, likewise strengthened American isolationist sentiments. In April, 1780, John Adams, continuing to take a suspicious view of the American association with Europe, wrote:

> Yet I have many reasons to think that not one of them, not even Spain nor France, wishes to see America rise very fast to power. We ought,

[6] *Treaties and Other International Acts of the United States,* ed. Hunter Miller (Washington, 1931–1948), II, 36–37.

[7] E. B. Greene, *The Revolutionary Generation, 1763–1790* (New York, 1943), 304.

therefore, to be cautious how we magnify our ideas, and exaggerate our expressions of the generosity and magnanimity of any of these powers. Let us treat them with gratitude, but with dignity. Let us remember what is due to ourselves and to our posterity, as well as to them. Let us, above all things, avoid as much as possible entangling ourselves with their wars or politics. Our business with them and theirs with us is commerce, not politics, much less war. America has been the sport of European wars and politics long enough.[8]

Therefore, by the time that Adams and John Jay reached Paris to join Franklin in negotiating the final peace terms in the Revolution, they had become more wary of France and Spain than of England. At the outset of the diplomatic discussions Adams wrote in his diary, "For my own part, I thought that America had been long enough involved in the wars of Europe. She had been a foot-ball between contending nations from the beginning, and it was easy to foresee that France and England both would endeavor to involve us in their future wars." He declared that he would lay down as a first principle of American foreign policy that

we should calculate all our measures and foreign negotiations in such a manner, as to avoid a too great dependence upon any one power of Europe—to avoid all obligations and temptations to take any part in future European wars; that the business of America with Europe was commerce, not politics or war. . . .

After the war, as the first diplomatic representative of the United States to Great Britain, Adams noted with approval the comment of the Swedish minister in London that he took it for granted that in America "you will have sense enough to see us in Europe cut each other's throats with a philosophical tranquility." Adams himself was convinced that "If all intercourse between Europe and America could be cut forever, if every ship we have were burnt, and the keel of another never laid, we might still be the happiest people on earth, and, in fifty years, the most powerful." [9]

Following the Revolution, Americans, in their disenchantment over the French alliance, came to feel that with independence secured foreign aid was no longer necessary. John Adams, for example, believed that the signing of the peace treaty made the United

8 *Works of John Adams*, VII, 151.
9 *Ibid.*, III, 308, VIII, 35, 178, 357.

States "independent of France, in point of moral and political ob-ligation." [10] "The true interest of the States," according to a resolu-tion adopted by the Continental Congress in 1783, "requires that they should be as little as possible entangled in the politics and controversies of European nations. . . ." [11] Echoing this view, George Washington, in a letter to a French friend in 1788, remarked: "Separated as we are by a world of water from other Nations, if we are wise we shall surely avoid being drawn into the labyrinth of their politics, and involved in their destructive wars." [12]

American self-confidence after the war was also bolstered by the way in which the United States had been able to gain the advantage at the peace table from the conflicting French, Spanish, and English desires in the New World. Franklin, Adams, and Jay had used well the diplomatic arts of a small nation against the interests of the large ones. Thus for many Americans the word "forever" in the French alliance of 1778 was not, as Alexander DeConde points out, "to be measured by the glass of time, but by convenience and neces-sity. With independence a fact, the French alliance was no longer needed; it was an embarrassing nuisance." [13]

Behind the strong isolationist views of Adams and many of the Founding Fathers lay their concern for the preservation of American freedom and security in its new nationalist state. Accordingly, when the future of the Republic seemed in jeopardy during the trouble-some period of domestic strife and confusion under the Articles of Confederation, a number of American political leaders actively sought to supplant the weak Articles with a stronger frame of gov-ernment. Domestic discontents, as illustrated by Shays' Rebellion, were a menace to the safety of the Republic both at home and abroad. After all, the United States could hardly command the respect of foreign powers unless it established a strong national gov-

[10] *Ibid.*, VIII, 235.

[11] *Journals of the Continental Congress, 1774–1789*, Gaillard Hunt, ed. (Washington, 1904–1937), XXIV, 394.

[12] *Writings of George Washington*, J. C. Fitzpatrick, ed. (Washington, 1931–1944), XXIX, 406.

[13] Alexander DeConde, *Entangling Alliance* (Durham, N.C., 1958), 15.

ernment. As John Jay, Secretary for Foreign Affairs during most of the Confederation period, pointed out, "To be respectable abroad, it is necessary to be so at home; and that will not be the case until our public faith acquires more confidence and our government more strength." [14]

Blessed with a natural geographic advantage by reason of its isolated position, the United States, as Hamilton, Jay, and Madison noted repeatedly in *The Federalist*, enjoyed a high degree of security without the expense of maintaining a large military establishment. "If we are wise enough to preserve the Union," Hamilton wrote, "we may for ages enjoy an advantage similar to that of an insulated situation. Europe is at a great distance from us. Her colonies in our vicinity will be likely to continue too much disproportioned in strength to be able to give us any dangerous annoyance. Extensive military establishments cannot, in this position, be necessary to our security." Liberty and national unity, rather than military measures, were the keys to the security of the Republic. "By a steady adherence to the Union, we may hope, erelong, to become the arbiter of Europe in America, and may be able to incline the balance of European competitions in this part of the world as our interest may dictate. . . . Let the thirteen States, bound together in a strict and indissoluble Union, concur in erecting one great American system, superior to the control of all transatlantic force or influence, and able to dictate the terms of the connection between the old and the new world!" [15]

Although Hamilton was optimistic in his view that the infant United States could set the terms of Europe's interest in the New World, the American continents were able nevertheless to profit from Europe's embroilment in the wars that were an outcome of the French Revolution. In an age of democratic revolution, the republics of North and South America stood to gain by their national independence. It is true that the United States quickly found itself involved in the conflict of the French and British empires—chiefly because of its desire to reap the benefits of wartime trade—but full-scale warfare was avoided until 1812. Meanwhile, it seemed to most

[14] *Correspondence and Public Papers of John Jay*, H. P. Johnston, ed. (New York, 1890–1893), III, 206.

[15] Alexander Hamilton, *The Federalist*, Nos. 8, 11, E. M. Earle, ed. (New York, 1937), 40, 65, 69.

Americans the better part of national wisdom to use the European wars as an opportunity to consolidate American independence. Yet few Americans were truly neutral in their view of the French Revolution, or of the European wars which followed. Taking sides in Europe, however, also meant taking sides in the United States. Thus Washington, Adams, Hamilton, and the Federalist party in general soon became bitterly hostile to the new French radical regime, while the Republican party followers of Jefferson and Madison, in contrast, viewed both the French Revolution and French pleas for American aid with open approval and sympathy.

With American opinion so sharply divided respecting the situation in Europe, a foreign policy that stressed peace and neutrality made good sense. In the fall of 1792, when there again seemed to be the danger of a rupture in American relations with Spain, and Alexander Hamilton suggested an alliance with England, Washington, according to Jefferson's recollection, replied that "the remedy would be worse than the disease." [16] Some months later, after receipt of the news of the British declaration of war against France, Washington expressed the hope that the United States would be able to stay out of the European conflict.[17]

A major crisis in American foreign policy at this time resulted from the interference in American domestic affairs of the French ministers to the United States. The Jeffersonians lent their enthusiasm to the diplomatic mission of Citizen Genêt partly because they felt the United States should continue to honor the Treaty of 1778, but also because they feared English influence upon the Federalists. The Federalists, on the other hand, were apprehensive lest the Republicans push the country into war against England. In this hotbed of domestic factionalism Washington's Proclamation of Neutrality, calling for friendly and impartial treatment of all belligerents, asserted an American national policy which the country generally came to accept. Jefferson, for example, though dubious of the wisdom of making such a public pronouncement, did not question peace and neutrality as desirable aims of American foreign policy.

Despite America's proclaimed neutrality, war with one or more of the European nations remained an ever-present hazard. American

---

[16] *Writings of Thomas Jefferson*, Memorial Edition, A. A. Lipscomb and A. E. Bergh, eds. (Washington, 1903), I, 323.

[17] *Writings of George Washington*, XXXII, 399.

interest in territorial expansion, particularly in Florida and New Orleans, and the desire to preserve a growing foreign trade with both England and France were goals that endangered the national policy of political and military isolation. In the series of diplomatic crises that followed in the wake of the French Revolution, the political and economic aspirations of the United States were accordingly in almost continual conflict, the one nullifying the other. For example, long-standing difficulties in the post-Revolutionary relations of England and the United States, threatening to lead the two countries into war, were only partially resolved by ratification of the unpopular Jay Treaty. Relations with France after 1793 also deteriorated—finally to the point of the undeclared naval war of 1798—before President Adams was able to work out a settlement in the Convention of 1800. By this new agreement, the French Treaty of 1778 was ended, thus freeing the United States of any direct alliance with a foreign power until the Second World War.

The classic statement of early American foreign policy, asserting views which endured for more than a century in the conduct of American diplomacy, was, of course, Washington's Farewell Address. Though modern historians have demonstrated the partisan political motives underlying Washington's pronouncement, noting especially Alexander Hamilton's role in helping to draft the address, the fact remains that Washington's advice in respect to the proper conduct of American foreign policy was, in general, adhered to by his successors. Whether Washington and later Presidents regarded their foreign policy as one of complete isolation may be doubted, but there is little reason to question the traditional idea that the United States conceived its national interests to be best served by avoiding entanglement in European affairs. As Dexter Perkins has noted, "during the first hundred odd years of this country's history, the isolationist point of view corresponded with the interests of the United States, with the realities of international intercourse, and even with American ideals." [18]

The familiar words of Washington stated not only a foreign policy for the young Republic, but also a broad national ideal which for at least a century defined American interests. Fearful of both the internal and external dangers that seemed to beset the American experiment in self-government, and concerned to "prevent our na-

[18] Perkins, *The American Approach to Foreign Policy*, 11.

tion from running the course which has hitherto marked the destiny of nations," Washington counseled:

> Observe good faith and justice toward all nations. Cultivate peace and harmony with all. . . .
>
> Against the insidious wiles of foreign influence . . . the jealousy of a free people ought to be *constantly* awake. . . . But that jealousy, to be useful, must be impartial. . . .
>
> Europe has a set of primary interests which to us have none or a very remote relation. . . .
>
> Our detached and distant situation invites and enables us to pursue a different course. . . .
>
> Why forego the advantages of so peculiar a situation? Why quit our own to stand upon foreign ground? Why, by interweaving our destiny with that of any part of Europe, entangle our peace and prosperity in the toils of European ambition, rivalship, interest, humor or caprice?
>
> It is our true policy to steer clear of permanent alliances with any portion of the foreign world, so far, I mean, as we are now at liberty to do it. . . .[19]

The foreign policy of the Washington and Adams administrations, as set forth in the Farewell Address and as practiced in Adams' about-face in the matter of war with France, kept the United States at peace, helping to consolidate the freedom and security of the Republic and preserving it alike from outside intervention and domestic insurrection. Moreover, the fundamental maxims in regard to foreign affairs delineated in Washington's Farewell Address were not reversed when the Jeffersonians came into political power. It continued to be the supreme national interest to keep America free and independent—a goal which Jefferson, like his predecessors, believed could best be attained by the pursuit of a policy of national isolation from Europe's wars.

When Thomas Jefferson became President in 1801, he was already the possessor of considerable experience in the conduct of American foreign affairs. As Minister to France for five years in suc-

[19] *A Compilation of the Messages and Papers of the Presidents, 1789–1897,* J. D. Richardson, ed. (Washington, 1896–1899), I, 221–223.

cession to Franklin, and then as Secretary of State under Washington, he had come into intimate contact with Europe. Like Franklin, he found much in Paris which was attractive to his civilized and sophisticated tastes. Traveling about the French countryside, he gathered books, art works, and furniture, as well as plants and seeds, to bring back with him to the United States. "Were I to proceed to tell you how much I enjoy their architecture, sculpture, painting, music," he wrote to the professor of modern languages at William and Mary, "I should want words." [20] Upon his return Jefferson applied his knowledge of European architecture to the construction of his home at Monticello, to the state capitol at Richmond, and to the first buildings of the University of Virginia. Despite the undoubted appeal of European life to his esthetic sense, however, his close observation of the political economy of the Old World reinforced his belief in the superiority of America. The rigid class society, monarchical governments, and concentration of the population in large cities all contributed to the decadence and corruption of the Old World. From the European nations the United States, he felt, should borrow only those ideas which would improve American cultural and economic life. Political and diplomatic connections, in contrast, should be limited strictly to such contacts and policies as might serve American national interests.

Ideally Jefferson would have preferred to see his countrymen confine themselves to agricultural pursuits, "to practise neither commerce nor navigation, but to stand, with respect to Europe, precisely on the footing of China. We should thus avoid wars, and all our citizens would be husbandmen." "I know, too," he wrote, "that it is a maxim with us, and I think it a wise one, not to entangle ourselves with the affairs of Europe." A weakness of the new United States Constitution, which he felt was second only to the lack of a bill of rights, was the failure to establish a firm principle of rotation in office, particularly in the case of the President. If, as he feared, the President could be constantly reelected, there would be an inducement on the part of foreign powers to "interfere with money and with arms" in the selection and policies of the American chief executive. On the other hand, "No foreign power, nor domestic party,

[20] *Papers of Thomas Jefferson*, J. P. Boyd, ed. (Princeton, 1950–   ), VIII, 569.

14 IDEAS, IDEALS, AND AMERICAN DIPLOMACY

will waste their blood and money to elect a person, who must go out at the end of a short period." [21]

Curiously enough, in this matter of the Presidency Jefferson's apprehensions came closest to realization in his own case. The improper interference of the French Minister Adet in urging Jefferson's election over John Adams in 1796 may have provoked just enough resentment among American voters to help insure the former's defeat. Successful four years later in an election in which French influence was conspicuously avoided, Jefferson in his Inaugural Address reasserted the American foreign policy of peace and neutrality. Alluding to the many advantages enjoyed by the Republic, including the separation from Europe "by nature and a wide ocean," Jefferson called for "Peace, commerce, and honest friendship with all nations, entangling alliances with none. . . ." [22]

To put into practice the political principles set forth in his Inaugural Address, Jefferson initiated rigid governmental economies which especially reduced the size and expense of the American military and diplomatic establishments. A man of peace, he nevertheless sanctioned a naval expedition against the Barbary pirates to stamp out their long-standing interference with American commerce in the Mediterranean. Despite the costs of the Barbary war, however, which were paid by increasing the tariff, the United States acted independently, without the cooperation of the European powers.

Most important of all the actions relating to foreign affairs in Jefferson's first administration was the purchase of Louisiana. Alarmed by the news of the transfer to France of this vast territory, Jefferson used the full force of his diplomacy to assert American national interests in the matter of the navigation of the Mississippi River. "The day that France takes possession of New Orleans, . . ." he wrote on April 18, 1802, "we must marry ourselves to the British fleet and nation." [23] Whether Jefferson actually intended to go this far in abandoning his own isolationist precepts of a proper American foreign policy is doubtful. But his threat was perhaps a useful diplomatic move which, fortunately, had never to be used since

[21] *Ibid.*, VIII, 633, XII, 441, 447; *Writings of Thomas Jefferson*, Memorial Ed., VI, 389–390.

[22] *Messages and Papers of the Presidents*, I, 323.

[23] *Writings of Thomas Jefferson*, Memorial Ed., X, 313.

Napoleon and the French, yielding their hopes of an empire in America, agreed to sell all Louisiana to the United States.

The major problem, and the essential tragedy, of Jefferson's Presidency was the great difficulty which he faced in keeping the country at peace. A young Republic whose swollen wartime commerce was prey to the rival ambitions of the great European coalitions led by England and France, the United States might easily have become entangled in the affairs of the Old World. That Jefferson was able to invoke the embargo policy in an effort to preserve American neutral rights without resort to war was partly a result of the new security of the American position which came from the purchase of Louisiana. In the words of Livingston and Monroe, the American diplomats who had received Napoleon's offer of Louisiana, by its acquisition "We separate ourselves in a great measure from the European world and its concerns, especially its wars and intrigues. We make, in fine, a great stride to real and substantial independence. . . ." [24] These extensive new lands west of the Mississippi, Jefferson himself believed, would keep the United States a nation of farmers, relieved of the necessity of cultivating any undue reliance on commerce or manufactures.

Thus the Louisiana Purchase was a boon to the economic and strategic position of the United States. It safeguarded future prosperity and may have postponed American involvement in the European war until 1812. In the view of a later historian, "The acquisition of Louisiana freed American statesmen from a fear which had been constantly recurring, and satisfied an appetite which might otherwise conceivably have led to dangerous political commitments. The consolidation of the nonentanglement idea may almost be said to date from 1803." [25]

Although James Madison, who followed Jefferson in the White House, was not able to continue successfully his predecessor's policies of peace and neutrality, the United States' entrance into the War of 1812 did not signify any weakening of the independent course of American diplomacy. With grievances against both France and England, the United States chose to war against the latter, not as an ally of Napoleon, but for its own national purposes. Neither

[24] *American State Papers, Foreign Relations* (Washington, 1832–1834), II, 559.

[25] Dexter Perkins, *A History of the Monroe Doctrine* (Boston, 1955), 20.

the American desire to protect its commerce nor the desire to gain territory in Canada indicated any wish to become embroiled in European politics. The war was rather a forcible reassertion of American independence and a protest against the British attempts to interfere with American sovereignty. In the opinion of Albert Gallatin, the former Secretary of the Treasury and one of the members of the American peace commission:

> The war has been productive of evil and good, but I think the good preponderates. . . . The war has renewed and reinstated the national feelings and character which the Revolution had given, and which were daily lessened. The people have now more general objects of attachment. . . . They are more Americans; they feel and act more as a nation; and I hope that the permanency of the Union is thereby better secured.[26]

According to Henry Adams, the biographer of Gallatin and the historian of the Jefferson and Madison administrations, "In 1815 for the first time Americans ceased to doubt the path they were to follow. Not only was the unity of their nation established, but its probable divergence from older societies was also well defined." [27]

The comments of Gallatin and Adams indicate the broader results of the War of 1812. In its protection of American sovereignty and in the strong nationalistic feelings which it generated, the struggle accomplished at least a part of its purpose. In this sense, therefore, it may properly be called the "second war for American independence."

With both economic and political independence assured after 1815, the ensuing "era of good feelings" in the United States was marked by a growing nationalistic spirit in foreign affairs. In these years America pursued an isolationist course, hating European despotism and sympathizing with the masses of the Old World in their attempts at revolution, but conscious of American differences and glad to have the chance to settle its own domestic policies with-

[26] *Writings of Albert Gallatin*, Henry Adams, ed. (Philadelphia, 1879), I, 700.

[27] Henry Adams, *History of the United States* (New York, 1889–1891), IX, 220.

out interference from Europe. This independent character of American diplomacy and the continuing disposition of the country to isolate itself from the Old World's quarrels received its classic expression in the Monroe Doctrine. President Monroe's pronouncement in 1823 was a formal statement of widespread American sentiments. It reflected the strong feeling of the American people against outside interference with life in the New World or with republican institutions. Three years before the Monroe Doctrine, Thomas Jefferson, for example, had already expressed the opinion:

> The day is not distant when we may formally require a meridian of partition through the ocean which separates the two hemispheres, on the hither side of which no European gun shall ever be heard, nor an American on the other; and when, during the rage of the eternal wars of Europe, the lion and the lamb, within our regions shall lie down together in peace. . . . The principles of society there and here, then are radically different, and I hope no American patriot will ever lose sight of the essential policy of interdicting in the seas and territories of both Americas, the ferocious and sanguinary contests of Europe.[28]

Whatever the outcome of the Latin American revolts and in whatever form of government they ended, Jefferson rejoiced that

> they will be *American* governments, no longer to be involved in the never ceasing broils of Europe. The European nations constitute a separate division of the globe; their localities make them a part of a distinct system; they have a set of interests of their own in which it is our business never to engage ourselves. America has a hemisphere to itself. It must have its separate system of interests; which must not be subordinated to those of Europe. The insulated state in which nature has placed the American continent, should so far prevail that no spark of war kindled in the other quarters of the globe should be wafted across the wide oceans which separate us from them. And it will be so.

When Jefferson was asked by President Monroe for his advice on the British proposal for some kind of joint Anglo-American warning to the European nations to refrain from intervention in South America, his reply was a reassertion of his isolationist beliefs:

> Our first and fundamental maxim should be, never to entangle ourselves in the broils of Europe. Our second, never to suffer Europe to in-

<hr>

[28] *Writings of Thomas Jefferson*, Memorial Ed., XV, 263.

termeddle in cis-Atlantic affairs. America, North and South, has a set of interests distinct from those of Europe, and peculiarly her own. She should therefore have a system of her own, separate and apart from that of Europe.

It was the very depth of Jefferson's isolationist feelings which led him to advise acceptance of the British proposal. Great Britain, "the nation which can do us the most harm of any one, of all on earth," would in this way, he hoped, be detached from the concert of European powers. And the Americas, in turn, would be better protected from involvement in European affairs.[29]

Unlike Jefferson, John Quincy Adams, President Monroe's Secretary of State, opposed any joint pronouncement with Great Britain. More clearly than Jefferson, Adams saw that the very power of Great Britain placed her in competition with the United States. The younger Adams, like his father, held staunch isolationist views in regard to American foreign policy. An experienced diplomat, John Quincy Adams became even more nationalistic and anti-European than either his father or Jefferson. In a dispatch to the American Minister in Russia, in explaining why the United States could not consider an invitation to join the Holy Alliance, Adams stated the view that

> The political system of the United States, is also essentially extra-European. To stand in firm and cautious independence of all entanglement in the European system has been a cardinal point of their policy under every administration of their government from the peace of 1783 to this day. . . . For the repose of Europe as well as of America, the European and American political systems should be kept as separate and distinct from each other as possible.[30]

Against President Monroe's idealistic disposition to issue a strong statement challenging the Holy Alliance and avowing American sympathy for the principles of national independence everywhere, however, Adams offered a counsel of moderation. Accordingly he opposed Monroe's sentimental desire to aid the cause of Greek independence—a step which would have inevitably entangled America in European affairs.

29 *Ibid.*, XIV, 22, XV, 477.
30 *Writings of John Quincy Adams*, W. C. Ford, ed. (New York, 1913–1917), VII, 49.

The fundamental goal of American policy, Adams believed, was the protection of the independence and security of the United States and of those territories in the New World which lay within the range of its primary interest. For more than thirty years, he pointed out, Europe had been in a state of war and revolution. Now if under the Holy Alliance, the reactionary European powers proposed to intervene in South America, the United States would "have as much as we can do to prevent them, without going to bid them defiance in the heart of Europe. . . . The ground that I wish to take is that of earnest remonstrance against the interference of the European powers by force with South America but to disclaim all interference with Europe; to make an American cause and adhere inflexibly to that." [31]

Although President Monroe did not conceal his sympathies for oppressed peoples everywhere, the final draft of his famous message conformed to Adams' isolationist advice. Like the earlier statements of Washington and Jefferson, the Monroe Doctrine asserted as the foundation principle of American foreign policy the concept of a separation of interests on the part of America and Europe. In the words of Monroe's well-known message:

. . . the American continents, by the free and independent condition which they have assumed and maintain, are henceforth not to be considered as subjects for future colonization by any European powers. . . .

In the wars of the European powers in matters relating to themselves we have never taken any part, nor does it comport with our policy so to do. . . .

We owe it, therefore, to candor and to the amicable relations existing between the United States and those powers to declare that we should consider any attempt on their part to extend their system to any portion of this hemisphere as dangerous to our peace and safety. With the existing colonies or dependencies of any European power we have not interfered and shall not interfere. But with the Governments who have declared their independence and maintained it, and whose independence we have, on great consideration and on just principles, acknowledged, we could not view any interposition for the purpose of oppressing them, or controlling in any other manner their destiny, by any European power in any other light than as the manifestation of an unfriendly disposition toward the United States. . . .

[31] *Memoirs of John Quincy Adams*, C. F. Adams, ed. (Philadelphia, 1874–1877), VI, 197–198.

Our policy in regard to Europe, which was adopted at an early stage of the wars which have so long agitated that quarter of the globe, nevertheless remains the same, which is, not to interfere in the internal concerns of any of its powers; to consider the government *de facto* as the legitimate government for us; to cultivate friendly relations with it, and to preserve those relations by a frank, firm, and manly policy, meeting in all instances the just claim of every power, submitting to injuries from none.[32]

First conceived as a stopgap measure in the face of the British offer of a joint statement of policy, the Monroe Doctrine was both an example of American nationalism and a warning to Europe. Negatively it reaffirmed the isolation of the American continents; positively it asserted the pretensions of the United States to a supranationalistic position of superiority and dominance in the New World. In general the Doctrine was the result of forces gradually building up within the United States, while the threatened interference of the Holy Alliance in South America furnished the immediate occasion for its pronouncement. From a detailed study of its background, E. H. Tatum has concluded that by 1823 "the trend of American thought and experience had been so definitely in the direction of an independent, national, republican foreign policy that a formal statement of it was inevitable. Sooner or later it would have been made. All that was necessary was a provocative 'incident.' " [33] Finally, it may be said that the group of ideas expressed in Monroe's passage prevailed because they stated important American interests in respect to foreign affairs.

The development and assertion of an independent foreign policy, separate from that of Europe and based on United States national interests, was the major diplomatic accomplishment of the first generation of American statesmen. Although this political isolationism remained a basic theme in the mainstream of foreign policy, there were other concepts which also contributed to the diverse currents of thought in American diplomacy. Isolationism was in itself evidence not only of American self-interest, but also of a strong underlying national idealism, and much of the early thinking of Americans in regard to foreign affairs reflected this philosophy. Confident of the uniqueness and merit of their political

---

[32] *Messages and Papers of the Presidents,* II, 209, 218–219.
[33] E. H. Tatum, *The United States and Europe* (Berkeley, Calif., 1936), 251.

institutions, the American people did not wish to have them sullied or endangered by the corrupting influence of the Old World. At the same time, however, many Americans, both officially and unofficially, also believed that the United States had a responsibility and a mission to make known to the peoples of the rest of the world the unprecedented advantages enjoyed by the American Republic. "The United States," President Monroe declared in his annual message to Congress in 1822, "owe to the world a great example, and, by means thereof, to the cause of liberty and humanity a generous support." [34] Thus isolationism and the doctrine of an American mission, though sometimes in conflict, were not entirely incompatible concepts of foreign policy. Both were, in part, complementary components of the early American dreams of Utopia and future progress.

SELECTED REFERENCES

Bemis, Samuel F. *John Quincy Adams and the Foundations of American Foreign Policy*. New York: Knopf, 1949.

Brown, Roger H. *The Republic in Peril: 1812*. New York: Columbia University Press, 1964.

DeConde, Alexander. *Entangling Alliance: Politics and Diplomacy under George Washington*. Durham N. C.: Duke University Press, 1958.

Gilbert, Felix. *To the Farewell Address: Ideas of Early American Foreign Policy*. Princeton: Princeton University Press, 1961.

Perkins, Dexter. *A History of the Monroe Doctrine*. Boston: Little, Brown, 1955.

Rippy, J. Fred. *America and the Strife of Europe*. Chicago: University of Chicago Press, 1938.

——— and Angie Debo, "The Historical Background of the American Policy of Isolation," *Smith College Studies in History*, Vol. IX. Northampton, Mass., 1924.

Stourzh, Gerald. *Benjamin Franklin and American Foreign Policy*. Chicago: University of Chicago Press, 1954.

Tatum, Edward H. *The United States and Europe, 1815–1823: A Study in the Background of the Monroe Doctrine*. Berkeley, Calif.: University of California Press. 1936.

Varg, Paul H. *Foreign Policies of the Founding Fathers*. East Lansing: Michigan State University Press, 1963.

[34] *Messages and Papers of the Presidents*, II, 194.

II

The Idea of Mission

The idea of a unique American mission has been an important theme in United States foreign policy. More than most nationalities, Americans have thought of themselves as destined to bring the blessings of liberty and self-government to the less fortunate parts of the world. Although this sense of mission has been particularly strong in American history, from earliest times other nations, too, have considered themselves as in some way chosen peoples. The belief of each country that it is endowed with a certain moral superiority entitling it to lead the rest of the world along the paths of light and rectitude is thus a very old one. The Hebrews, for example, regarded themselves as persons favored by God, while to the ancient Greeks the remaining inhabitants of the world were uncivilized barbarians.

Long before the achievement of American independence, settlers in the thirteen Colonies were already impressed with the great and providential advantages which they enjoyed. Thus the early Puritans on their way westward across the Atlantic in the spring of 1630 were indulged with a hopeful prophecy in a sermon preached by their leader John Winthrop. "Wee shall be," Winthrop told his fellow passengers, "as a Citty upon a Hill, the eies of all people are uppon us; soe that if wee shall deal falsely with our god in this worke wee have undertaken and soe cause him to withdraw his present help from us, wee shall be made a story and a by-word through the world." "No one writing after the fact, three hundred years later," Daniel Boorstin remarks, "could better have expressed the American sense of destiny." [1] In New England the Puritans, in

[1] *Winthrop Papers* (Boston, 1929–1931), II, 295; D. J. Boorstin, *The Americans: The Colonial Experience* (New York, 1958), 3–4.

realization of Winthrop's prediction, were able to establish a Bible Commonwealth in the wilderness which, they believed, by illustrating God's providence would serve as a model and inspiration to other less favored peoples.

Geography, climate, natural resources, and a growing population all indicated the rich and varied promise of the North American continent. Consequently, it seemed apparent to many observers that the world's best hopes for the future would lie in the areas to the west of the Atlantic. The very discovery of America and its rapid colonization were in themselves recognition of Europe's needs for new lands and markets. Speaking for this point of view, John Adams asserted in 1765 that he had always regarded the settlement of America "with reverance and wonder, as the opening of a grand scheme and design in Providence for the illumination of the ignorant, and the emancipation of the slavish part of mankind all over the earth." [2]

The natural support which the environment of the New World extended to the doctrine of a unique American mission was greatly enhanced by the political and social contributions of the American Revolution. English reformers and French *savants* as well as American political leaders were quick to see the events of 1776 as an example to the Old World. Poets and philosophers together with the common man paid tribute to the importance of the American revolt. Following the news of the French Alliance of 1778, Americans, in offering their toasts to Louis XVI as "the magnanimous protector of the rights of mankind," also expressed the hope that America's influence might inspire the oppressed everywhere to resist tyranny and secure their "natural and inalienable rights." [3] Philip Freneau, poet of the American Revolution, whose commencement ode at Princeton in 1771 was addressed to the theme "The Rising Glory of America," now seven years later celebrated in verse the importance of "America Independent."

[2] *Works of John Adams*, C. F. Adams, ed. (Boston, 1850–1856), I, 66.
[3] E. B. Greene, *The Revolutionary Generation, 1763–1790* (New York, 1943), 305.

America! the works of peace be thine,
Thus shalt thou gain a triumph more divine—
To thee belongs a second golden reign,
Thine is the empire o'er a peaceful main;
Protect the rights of human kind below
Crush the proud tyrant who becomes their foe,
And future times shall own your struggles blest,
And future years enjoy perpetual rest.
    Americans! revenge your countries wrongs;

• • •

Your mighty wrongs the tragic muse shall trace,
Your gallant deeds shall fire a future race;
To you may kings and potentates appeal,
You may the doom of jarring nations seal;
A glorious empire rises, bright and new!
Firm be the structure, and must rest on you! [4]

And in "An Oration on the Advantages of American Independence," David Ramsay, the future historian of the Revolution, declared:

Our independence will redeem one quarter of the globe from tyranny and oppression, and consecrate it the chosen seat of truth, justice, freedom, learning and religion. We are laying the foundation of happiness for countless millions. Generations yet unborn will bless us for the blood-bought inheritance we are about to bequeath them.[5]

The surprising success of the Revolution, dramatized in the battle at Yorktown and climaxed by the Treaty of 1783, made the new nation conscious of its unique position as a republic in a world of monarchies. Alone among the inhabitants of the world, Americans were granted the opportunity to construct their government with respect for the natural rights of man. The American people, therefore, had as their first responsibility the duty to make these rights secure at home. But it was also natural for Americans, despite their isolationist inclinations, to feel a bond of sympathy and concern for foreign peoples who still suffered from the effects of tyrannical governments. In 1782 with independence all but won, Benjamin Franklin, writing to the Chevalier de Chastellux, ventured to predict:

[4] Philip Freneau, *Poems Written and Published During the American Revolutionary War* (Philadelphia, 1809), I, 249–250.

[5] *United States Magazine,* I (March, 1779), 106.

Establishing the liberties of America will not only make that people happy, but will have some effect in diminishing the misery of those, who in other parts of the world groan under despotism, by rendering it more circumspect, and inducing it to govern with a lighter hand.[6]

In New England Ezra Stiles, President of Yale, chose as the title of his election sermon for 1783, "The United States Elevated to Glory and Honor." His country, Stiles declared, was "God's American Israel," an independent nation from which Europe and Asia would "hereafter learn that the most liberal principles of law and civil polity" as well as "the true religion" were "to be found on this side of the Atlantic," far removed from "the rust and corruption of ages." [7]

The confidence in the American political mission voiced by Franklin and Stiles at the conclusion of the Revolution was widely echoed over the years. John Adams predicted in 1785 that the United States was "destined beyond a doubt to be the greatest power on earth, and that within the life of man." [8] Washington, who on occasion called himself "A Citizen of the great republic of humanity at large," declared as President that "the preservation of the sacred fire of liberty" depended "on the experiment intrusted to the hands of the American people." [9] Jefferson meanwhile termed a "just and solid republican government . . . a standing monument and example for the aim and imitation of the people of other countries. . . ." [10] Joel Barlow, more radical than his fellow Connecticut Wits, in his long epic poem "The Vision of Columbus," set forth the happy idea that the great explorer's hopes for the future were now to be realized as a result of the American Revolution. Not only did the Revolution assure the future progress of the American people, but its benefits would also be extended in time to the rest of the earth.

[6] *Writings of Benjamin Franklin*, A. H. Smyth, ed. (New York, 1905–1907), VIII, 416.

[7] Quoted in Cushing Strout, *The American Image of the Old World* (New York, 1963), 16.

[8] *Works of John Adams*, VIII, 246.

[9] *Writings of George Washington*, J. C. Fitzpatrick, ed. (Washington, 1931–1944), XXVIII, 520; *A Compilation of the Messages and Papers of the Presidents, 1789–1897*, J. D. Richardson, ed. (Washington, 1896–1899), I, 53.

[10] *Writings of Thomas Jefferson*, Memorial Edition, A. A. Lipscomb and A. E. Bergh, eds. (Washington, 1903), X, 217.

> See, thro' the whole, the same progressive plan,
> That draws for mutual succor, man to man,
> From friends to tribes, from tribes to realms ascend,
> Their powers, their interests and their passions blend;
>
>   •   •   •
>
> Till tribes and states and empires find their place,
> And one wide interest sways the peaceful race.[11]

In their correspondence, in sermons and addresses, and especially in the patriotic speeches which they made each Fourth of July, the American people celebrated the influence of the Revolution and its probable effect upon the destinies of the other nations of the globe. The reformation of less favored countries was to be the mission of America, and the duty held out to the people of the United States as a result of the success of their own Revolution. In the words of the historian George Bancroft:

> The authors of the American Revolution avowed for their object the welfare of mankind, and believed that they were in the service of their own and of all future generations. Their faith was just; for the world of mankind does not exist in fragments, nor can a country have an isolated existence. All men are brothers; and all are bondsmen for one another. All nations, too, are brothers, and each is responsible for that federative humanity which puts the ban of exclusion on none. New principles of government could not assert themselves in one hemisphere without affecting the other. The very idea of the progress of an individual people, in its relation to universal history, springs from the acknowledged unity of the race.[12]

While Americans understandably regarded their Revolution as an inspiration to mankind, many European philosophers and statesmen were just as eager to pay tribute to the influence and example of the War for Independence of the thirteen Colonies. "The first and greatest effect of the American Revolution in Europe," writes Robert R. Palmer, "was to make Europeans believe, or rather feel, often in a highly emotional way, that they lived in a rare era of momentous change. . . . The American Revolution coincided with the climax of the Age of Enlightenment. It was itself, in some degree, the product of this age. . . . It proved that the liberal ideas of

---

[11] Joel Barlow, *The Vision of Columbus* (Hartford, 1787), 240–241.
[12] George Bancroft, *History of the United States* (Boston, 1834–1874), IV, 5–6.

the Enlightenment might be put into practice." "Thus early in the war," another scholar points out, "American liberty came to signify to most Frenchmen not merely an overthrow of the British political and economic control, but a revolt of an entire people against the tyranny of an absolute power, a mass assertion of the inalienable rights of man." [13]

French liberals, looking toward the reformation of their own country, saw in the events across the Atlantic a harbinger of a new era. Thus they welcomed the news of the American protests against Britain and the outbreak of the Revolution. The French Finance Minister, Turgot, who had prudently opposed French economic aid to the United States and who also disapproved of certain features of the new American state constitutions, nevertheless expressed the wish that the American people "may attain the prosperity of which they are susceptible. They are the hope of the human race; they may well become its model." Less qualified in his enthusiasm than Turgot, Condorcet, the liberal *philosophe*, published in 1786 a remarkable essay entitled "The Influence of the American Revolution on Europe." Progress, Condorcet believed, would be achieved only through the realization of the principles of the Enlightenment, and America was now a living proof of these universal truths: "It is not enough that the rights of man be written in the books of philosophers and inscribed in the hearts of virtuous men; the weak and ignorant must be able to read them in the example of a great nation. America has given us this example." Moreover, "despite the differences of climate, tradition and constitution, the spectacle of a great nation where the rights of man are respected demonstrates that these rights are universal to all peoples." [14]

At a time when the outbreak of the French Revolution was arousing the anxiety of an old British Whig like Edmund Burke, it was, however, also touching off the celebrations of those who saw the events in France as a demonstration of the successful influence of the American revolutionary mission. In France Mirabeau and Lafayette

[13] R. R. Palmer, *The Age of the Democratic Revolution* (Princeton, 1959–1964), I, 239; Durand Echeverria, *Mirage in the West* (Princeton, 1957), 70.
[14] Quoted in Echeverria, *Mirage in the West*, 69, 153.

appealed to their fellow citizens to follow the American example, and the French Declaration of the Rights of Man expressed the same desire for liberty that was characteristic of the American declarations and constitutions. From America Tom Paine and Joel Barlow came to Paris to join in the new revolutionary cause, and Barlow later died in Poland in the midst of Napoleon's retreat from Russia.

Paine, whose *Common Sense* had been translated into French, accepted the outbreak of 1789 as the logical continuation of the struggle for the rights of man which had been inaugurated in the thirteen Colonies. Penning his *Rights of Man* in answer to Burke's *Reflections,* Paine rejoiced that "The opinions of men with respect to government are changing fast in all countries. The revolutions of America and France have thrown a beam of light over the world, which reaches into man." In contrast to the way in which the peoples of Europe still suffered the costs of monarchy, Paine wrote:

> I see in America the generality of people living in a style of plenty unknown in monarchical countries; and I see that the principle of its government, which is that of the *equal Rights of Man,* is making rapid progress in the world. . . .

Paine emphasized the continuity of the two revolutions by dedicating the first part of his work to Washington and the second part to Lafayette. America, he believed, would be the scene of a coming reformation of the world, and he concluded:

> From the rapid progress which America makes in every species of movement, it is rational to conclude that, if the governments of Asia, Africa, and Europe had begun on a principle similar to that of America, or had not been very early corrupted, therefrom, those countries must by this time have been in a far superior condition to what they are.

The French and American Revolutions offered the rest of the world an opportunity to embrace freedom which, if taken, would mean that "The present age will hereafter merit to be called the Age of Reason, and the present generation will appear to the future as the Adam of a new world." [15]

While the French Revolution could be regarded as a reflection of the American, the latter, in turn, took on added significance after its example reached abroad. At the same time there was the possi-

[15] *Writings of Thomas Paine,* M. D. Conway, ed. (New York, 1906–1908), II, 359, 367, 402.

bility that a collapse of the Revolutionary movement in France might encourage reactionary elements in their distrust of democracy in the United States. "I feel," Thomas Jefferson wrote in discussing the two revolutions in August, 1791, "that the permanence of our own leans in some degree on that, and that a failure there would be a powerful argument to prove there would be a failure here." [16]

In the United States, for a brief period, enthusiasm over the French Revolution was almost as marked among conservatives as among liberals or radicals like Paine and Barlow. Americans generally rejoiced in the spread of the principles of self-government. A constitutional regime in place of an absolute monarchy was regarded as the triumph of the American example and as the fulfillment of the liberal teachings of Franklin and Jefferson during their services as Ministers in Paris. In the *Gazette of the United States* the conservative Federalist editor, John Fenno, inspired by the news of impending reforms in the French Government, wrote in 1789:

> The Revolution of America, it was very clearly predicted, would have a great influence upon the public affairs of the European world, but the most sanguine advocates for the liberties of mankind could not have anticipated those surprising events, which have already transpired to distinguish the annals of the present age. Our generous and magnanimous ally, the French nation, in their publications upon laws, government and Freedom discover a noble ardor in the best of causes, and the following communication will show that under the best of Kings they are on the eve of establishing a new and free Constitution.[17]

"But frenzies do not last, and enthusiasms wane. The democracy might sing Ça Ira, but the machinery of government was nonetheless in the hands of the Hamiltonians—that is to say of the upper class, and the upper class did not look with favor on the revolution." Thus Howard Mumford Jones describes the quick change in American opinion which followed the news of the execution of Louis XVI and Marie Antoinette and the Reign of Terror in France. "The French Revolution ceased to be a distant adventure and became for many a menace and a danger." [18]

[16] *Writings of Thomas Jefferson,* Memorial Ed., VIII, 234.

[17] *Gazette of the United States,* April 18, 1789, in Bernard Faÿ, *The Revolutionary Spirit in France and America* (New York, 1927), 272.

[18] H. M. Jones, *America and French Culture, 1750–1848* (Chapel Hill, 1927), 538–539.

Looking back on these years from the vantage point of their long experience, John Adams and Thomas Jefferson later summed up their varied reactions to the possibility that the French Revolution might encourage the Old World to follow in the footsteps of the United States and fulfill the promise of the American mission. Adams, the conservative Federalist, was dubious from the beginning about the radical program in France. Believing that Europe by the close of the eighteenth century was "advancing by slow but sure steps towards an amelioration of the condition of man in religion and government, in liberty, equality, fraternity, knowledge, civilization, and humanity," Adams in a letter of 1813 to Jefferson went on to say: "The French Revolution I dreaded, because I was sure it would not only arrest the progress of improvement, but give it a retrograde course, for at least a century, if not many centuries." The political opponent of Adams on most public questions, Jefferson combined an international outlook with a liberal faith that the United States would be the theater of the world's future progress. Undiscouraged by such periodic retrograde motions as seemed to be taking place in the Napoleonic period, Jefferson predicted to Adams in 1816:

We are destined to be a barrier against the returns of ignorance and barbarism. Old Europe will have to lean on our shoulders, and to hobble along by our side, under the monkish trammels of priests and kings, as she can. What a colossus shall we be, when the southern continent comes up to our mark! What a stand will it secure as a ralliance for the reason and freedom of the globe! I like the dreams of the future better than the history of the past.[19]

Adams' consistent skepticism and Jefferson's growing disillusionment over the French Revolution strengthened their mutual feelings that the world's hopes for the future would have to rest with the United States. Despite the temporary setback in France and the growing reactionary spirit in England, Americans still believed that it was the destiny of free institutions to overcome despotism. Faith in the American mission accordingly was not immediately impaired by the collapse of liberalism in France. For Jefferson the principles of 1776, commemorated each Fourth of July in the United States, continued to be the "grounds of hope for others." In the

---

[19] *Writings of Thomas Jefferson*, Memorial Ed., XIII, 314, XV, 58–59.

last letter of his life, two weeks before his own death and that of
John Adams on the fiftieth anniversary of the signing of the Declaration of Independence, Jefferson voiced the hope that this day may
"be to the world, what I believe it will be (to some parts sooner,
to others later, but finally to all), the signal of arousing men to
burst the chains under which monkish ignorance and superstition
had persuaded them to bind themselves, and to assume the blessings
and security of self-government." [20]

Although the principles of the American and French Revolutions had not been able to prevent the conservative reaction that
followed Napoleon's despotism, the course of events in Europe provided the opportunity for the peoples of Hispanic America to rise
against Spain. Despite some initial confusion in the United States
as to the meaning of the revolts, public opinion was generally sympathetic. Americans were naturally pleased to think that sister republics to the south were following their example. And it also
comported with American isolationism to be able to contrast the
despotism of the Old World with the rise of self-government in the
New. Indeed, what was more logical than that United States missionary influence should win its first converts in the other American
continent? Unofficial aid despite a United States neutrality act, and
optimistic expectations of trade and commerce, culminated in a
growing popular demand that the Government in Washington extend immediate recognition to the Latin American republics. Henry
Clay, the leader of this movement in Congress, suggested that the
independent republics of the two Americas might form "a sort of
counterpoise to the holy alliance . . . to operate by the force of example and moral influence. . . ."[21] But Clay, despite his interest in
recognition, did not advocate that North American aid be extended
to include military intervention or assistance.

A prominent figure among the War Hawks of 1812, Clay spoke

[20] *The Life and Selected Writings of Thomas Jefferson,* Adrienne Koch and
William Peden, eds. (New York, 1944), 729.

[21] Speech, Lexington, May 19, 1821, in A. P. Whitaker, *The United States
and the Independence of Latin America* (Baltimore, 1941), 345.

for the traditional hostility of the American West to the empires of Spain and England. In contrast to Clay, however, the Monroe administration and especially its Secretary of State, John Quincy Adams, were by no means so sure that the destiny of the United States was intertwined with the revolutionary cause of Latin America. Adams accordingly persuaded President Monroe to withhold recognition of the new republics until the United States had safely negotiated the acquisition of Florida from Spain. Thus the idea of a mission to spread democracy to the world came into conflict with the United States's own territorial ambitions, and in the case of Latin America versus Florida the former had to defer to the latter. According to Adams's definition of the American mission, the United States "goes not abroad in search of monsters. She is the well-wisher to the freedom and independence of all. She is the champion and vindicator only of her own." [22]

After Florida was secured in 1821, the United States finally recognized the independence of the American republics. In subsequent years, some of the political ideas of North America continued to exert considerable influence upon the neighboring republics to the south, and the diplomats sent out by the United States were instructed to explain the merits of democracy to their hosts. On the whole, however, trade in neither ideas nor goods was great between the American continents, and two United States envoys to Latin America—Joel Roberts Poinsett and William Henry Harrison—were given their passports because of their aggressiveness in promoting liberal political programs.

The Monroe Doctrine itself, especially in contrast to Clay's notion of some kind of united American front against the Holy Alliance, was essentially negative—a unilateral pronouncement by the United States of a nationalistic, isolationist policy. Moreover, the destiny of the United States, in the sense of the peaceful workings of the American mission, seemed to point more to Europe than to South America. In the New World, after all, the United States had pretensions of its own which were not always in harmony with the interests of the Latin American republics and which were also not to be satisfied merely by the peaceful demonstration of the American example. Finally, as the prospects for trade with Latin America

[22] Fourth of July Oration, 1821, *Niles' Weekly Register*, XX (July 21, 1821), 331.

failed to come up to expectations and as a number of the South American republics fell under the sway of military dictators, United States interest and hopes for democracy in Hispanic America declined abruptly.

In Europe, in contrast to Latin America, Americans were able to take heart from the gradual revival of the democratic movement after its eclipse in the years before and after 1815. Mass uprisings, motivated by liberal desires for national self-determination and political and economic reforms, spread across the Continent. Greeks, Poles, Belgians, Frenchmen, Italians, Germans, and Hungarians all rose in revolts which aroused the popular feelings and sympathy of the United States.

American public opinion was especially stirred by the revolt of the Greeks against their Turkish rulers in 1821. The so-called "Greek fever," stimulated by stories of Turkish atrocities, aroused the American conscience. A romantic interest on the part of college students and classical scholars was matched by mass meetings throughout the United States, and prominent American statesmen, including President Monroe, became warm advocates of the Greek cause. As the movement for American aid came to a head in late 1823 and early 1824, a resolution in favor of Greek independence was offered in Congress, and funds were raised from the American people to support the revolutionary struggle. But official United States action was confined to expressions of sympathetic concern for the embattled Greeks.

The revolutionary movement in Europe also achieved some success when, in 1830, the peoples of Belgium gained their national independence and the French substituted the liberal July monarchy of Louis Philippe for the conservative regime of Charles X. In Belgium revolutionary leaders were inspired by the example of the American Revolution and Constitution. They also followed the American innovation of a separation of church and state in order to avoid conflict between the interests of the Catholic and the liberal parties, and years later one of the authors of this compromise, the Belgian priest Desiré de Haerne, in an address in the House of Representatives, declared to the American Congress:

We are the only nation that has remained faithful in spirit to traditional rights and has followed America from the foundation of her political establishment and her liberal institutions. Yes, we looked upon England, . . . but, at the same time, we were conscious that there were certain customs in the institutions of that country we could not adopt, and we cast our eyes beyond the Atlantic, where we found a great people worthy of our entire imitation, and it is the institutions of that people we have chiefly inscribed upon our organic charter. We have followed their example in all that regards public liberty, the distribution of power, the election of representatives and decentralization of rule.[23]

By the 1830's the American democratic mission appeared to be gaining its chief support in the two areas of the world that were probably the most closely related to the American people and institutions—Great Britain and Canada. The Canadian rebellion of 1837 challenged the enforcement of American neutrality along the border and caused many Americans to feel that their northern neighbors were ready at long last to join the United States in asserting independence from Great Britain. American sympathy with Canada was all the greater because of the number of annoying issues which continued to disturb diplomatic relations between the United States and England. While the United States government adhered officially to a neutral course, American volunteers and arms found their way across the boundary line before the Canadian revolt was suppressed.

Actually Americans were too much inclined to regard every manifestation of the Canadian people's political discontent as an indication that they desired to follow in the footsteps of the United States. In contrast, despite the generally antagonistic attitude of the British people and Government toward the United States and the widespread Anglo-phobia among the American people, the impact of American democracy was probably stronger in England in the middle of the nineteenth century than in any other country.

American influence was especially marked among English radicals who admired the example of the liberal suffrage, free press, religious liberty, and system of public education in the United States. English supporters of the Reform Bill of 1832 pointed in envy to the American democratic suffrage, and the English Chartists and work-

[23] Quoted in Halvdan Koht, *The American Spirit in Europe* (Philadelphia, 1949), 24.

ing class also used the example of the United States to win support for their economic and political program. Jeremy Bentham, the celebrated utilitarian and philosophic radical, admired Andrew Jackson's Presidential Administration and seemed to see in the American system the chief working illustration of many of his own principles. The American President, in turn, in concluding his Farewell Message asserted that Providence had chosen Americans "as the guardians of freedom to preserve it for the benefit of the human race." [24]

While English conservatives remained critical of American political and social institutions, many of the more liberal and radical elements in Britain were fearful only that the example of American liberty might be lost upon the rest of the world. Some segments of British radicalism believed that it was the American mission to liberate the world and remedy the general failure of the Revolutions of 1848 in Europe. As an example, the American reputation abroad was described in a somewhat exaggerated way by one writer in a small radical English newspaper, who exclaimed:

> An American force in the battlefield of Europe, raising the standard of Universal Democracy, would call forth every People of the Continent in hope, courage, and irresistible numbers. Floating in that field, "the star-spangled banner" would strike terror and despair into the heart of old Despotism, conscious of its doom. Its very coming would be victory.[25]

Although the Revolutions of 1848 were suppressed almost before the news of their beginnings could arouse American support, the Magyar revolt in Austria-Hungary and its leader Louis Kossuth particularly stirred American public opinion. Alone among the European revolutionary movements, the Hungarian cause created a demand in Congress for some form of American intervention. In contrast to France and Germany, where the Revolutions of 1848 were tinged with socialistic radicalism, the struggle of the Magyars for national self-determination seemed to follow more closely the pattern of the American Revolution. After Russian intervention helped suppress the Magyar rebellion, Kossuth was brought from his exile in Turkey to America. Greeted with tumultuous enthusiasm

[24] *Messages and Papers of the Presidents,* III, 308.
[25] *The Leader,* December 20, 1851, in G. D. Lillibridge, *Beacon of Freedom* (Philadelphia, 1955), 82.

as the Hungarian George Washington, Kossuth proceeded to campaign for American financial backing and for some form of recognition or intervention.

While no foreign visitor since Lafayette had received a warmer public welcome in the United States, Kossuth also soon learned to his dismay that the government in Washington had no intention of abandoning its official policy of nonintervention. Thus Secretary of State Daniel Webster rebuffed Austrian protests over American unneutrality with the boast that "the prevalence on the other continent of sentiments favorable to republican liberty is the result of the reaction of America upon Europe," but he also replied to the entreaties of Kossuth in the same rhetorical and evasive fashion.[26] Even Henry Clay, the once fiery War Hawk of 1812, and the early advocate of Latin American independence, now told Kossuth that he despaired of any immediate success for liberal movements in Europe. America would have to look to itself to keep alive the fires of freedom. "Far better is it for ourselves, for Hungary, and for the course of liberty," he said, "that adhering to our wise, pacific system, and avoiding the distant wars of Europe, we should keep our lamp burning brightly on this western shore as a light to all nations, than to hazard its utter extinction amid the ruins of fallen or falling republics in Europe."[27] United States policy, declared President Fillmore, "is wisely to govern ourselves, and thereby to set such an example of natural justice, prosperity, and true glory as shall teach to all nations the blessings of self-government and the unparalleled enterprise and success of a free people."[28]

As one European revolutionary movement after another failed, even the most enthusiastic American liberals were forced to admit that the American mission to advance the cause of world liberty would have to be confined for the present to the example of United States democracy at home. Only a small and radical group within the Democratic party in the early 1850's, the so-called "Young

[26] *Writings and Speeches of Daniel Webster,* National Edition (Boston, 1903), XII, 169.

[27] *Works of Henry Clay,* Calvin Colton, ed. (New York, 1904), III, 224.

[28] *Messages and Papers of the Presidents,* V, 180.

America" faction, attempted to keep alive the hope of American intervention in the political troubles of Europe. Although the Young America program received encouragement from Democratic politicians anxious to divert American attention from the slavery controversy, the notion of supporting revolution in Europe no longer seemed an appropriate part of the American mission. Americans had naturally desired to see the spread of their institutions abroad, but the very concept of the uniqueness of America and its Utopian character militated against the possibility of its easy export. As Cushing Strout points out in regard to the American impact on Europe, "If America was in truth a New World with an already liberalized society as a setting for its Revolution, then its direct relevance could not be realistically insisted upon...." [29]

In the case of Europe, the idea of an American mission continued to have an indirect connection with United States foreign policy in the sense of pride and confidence which Americans gained from the export of their technology and culture. Robert Fulton's steamboat, Samuel F. B. Morse's telegraph, and the successful use of anaesthesia to dull pain in medical and dental operations were examples of American inventive genius which enhanced the prestige of the United States abroad. The arrival of America on the stage of science and industry received further dramatic illustration when the United States made a creditable showing with its agricultural and mechanical exhibits at the first World's Fair in the Crystal Palace in London in 1851. In the United States the Commissioner of Patents in his *Report* referred to the praise won by American inventions as demonstrating "the progressiveness of the human mind when in the enjoyment of liberty." [30] Morse himself, hopeful that his invention might have true international significance, predicted optimistically at this time that one of the results of the telegraph would be to "bind man to his fellowman in such bonds of amity as to put an end to war." [31]

Although Americans had to endure much criticism for their supposed materialism and lack of culture as compared with the

[29] Strout, *The American Image of the Old World*, 60.

[30] *Report of the Commissioner of Patents 1851*, 32 Cong., 1 Sess., *House Ex. Docs. No. 102* (Washington, 1852), 485.

[31] *Letters and Journals of Samuel F. B. Morse*, E. L. Morse, ed. (Boston, 1914), II, 345.

peoples of the Old World, American writers, like American inventors, were beginning to win attention abroad. The popularity of Washington Irving's and James Fenimore Cooper's books in England was followed by the publication of other American works, including the poetry of Longfellow and Poe, and William Hickling Prescott's colorful histories of the colonial period in Spanish America. For many peoples, America continued to be a land of promise and opportunity, and its techniques of invention and mass production and the increasing reputation of its literature abroad probably did more to spread the example of American institutions than the possibility of United States intervention in the mid-century political upheavals of the Old World. The lesson of the New World to the Old was one of peaceful progress.

As the more cautious among American statesmen at the time of the Kossuth excitement realized, popular crusading zeal in support of the mission of American democracy could involve the United States in war with one or more of the European powers. In criticizing the Young America faction of the rival Democratic party, the conservative Whig President Millard Fillmore warned Congress that wars and revolutions designed to spread freedom might only result in its destruction. Affirming his belief that "we live in an age of progress, and ours is emphatically a country of progress," Fillmore invoked the force of this concept against those who mistook

change for progress and the invasion of the rights of others for national prowess and glory. The former are constantly agitating for some change in the organic law, or urging new and untried theories of human rights. The latter are ever ready to engage in any wild crusade against a neighboring people, regardless of the justice of the enterprise and without looking at the fatal consequences to ourselves and to the cause of popular government.[32]

The mission of America was a reflection of the sense of uniqueness of the country and its institutions. While such a nationalistic, Utopian concept gave strength and vitality to American foreign policy, it was also, as President Fillmore pointed out, not without its dangers. Feeling themselves different, it was convenient for Americans to believe that United States diplomacy should likewise be judged differently in the court of world opinion. As a recent

[32] *Messages and Papers of the Presidents,* V, 181.

scholarly critic has written, however, it was for too long easy for Americans to overlook "the ethical trap they were laying for themselves by the advocacy of this double standard. The constant evocation of uniqueness and moral superiority prepared the way for the dangerous doctrine that the ends justify the means." [33] In the war with Mexico, the American people largely embraced such a doctrine, justifying their aggressive nationalist expansionism in terms of what they called their "manifest destiny." Thus the considerable idealism which had motivated the earlier concept of an American mission was gradually transformed and transfused by the more self-centered doctrine of manifest destiny.

SELECTED REFERENCES

Burns, Edward M. *The American Idea of Mission: Concepts of National Purpose and Destiny.* New Brunswick N.J.: Rutgers University Press, 1957.

Echeverria, Durand. *Mirage in the West: A History of the French Image of American Society to 1815.* Princeton: Princeton University Press, 1957.

Ekirch, Arthur A. *The Idea of Progress in America, 1815–1860.* New York: Columbia University Press, 1944.

Faÿ, Bernard. *The Revolutionary Spirit in France and America.* New York: Harcourt, Brace, 1927.

Jones, Howard M. *America and French Culture, 1750–1848.* Chapel Hill: University of North Carolina Press, 1927.

Koht, Halvdan. *The American Spirit in Europe: A Survey of Transatlantic Influences.* Philadelphia: University of Pennsylvania Press, 1949.

Lillibridge, G. D. *Beacon of Freedom: The Impact of American Democracy upon Great Britain, 1830–1870.* Philadelphia: University of Pennsylvania Press, 1955.

Palmer, Robert R. *The Age of the Democratic Revolution: A Political History of Europe and America, 1760–1800.* 2 vols. Princeton: Princeton University Press, 1959–1964.

Strout, Cushing. *The American Image of the Old World.* New York: Harper & Row, 1963.

Whitaker, Arthur P. *The United States and the Independence of Latin America, 1800–1830.* Baltimore: John Hopkins Press, 1941.

[33] Charles Lerche, *Foreign Policy of the American People* (Englewood Cliffs, N.J., 1958), 181–182.

III

Manifest Destiny

The concept of manifest destiny is particularly associated in American history with the aggressive diplomacy of the 1840's. In this decade the continental limits of the United States were carried westward to the shores of the Pacific and as far south as the Rio Grande. The national domain was rounded out by the accession of vast and valuable territories, and the United States could be said to have achieved its "natural boundaries." Thus, in a short span of time, the United States had already moved to fulfill the prediction of Tocqueville, when he wrote:

At a period which may be said to be near,—for we are speaking of the life of a nation,—the Anglo-Americans alone will cover the immense space contained between the polar regions and the tropics, extending from the coasts of the Atlantic to those of the Pacific Ocean.[1]

The first widely noted use of the phrase "manifest destiny" seems to have occurred in 1845 in an editorial by John L. O'Sullivan in the *Democratic Review*. Under the title "Annexation," O'Sullivan declared that God had marked out Oregon, Texas, and the remaining continental territories for possession by the United States. Even though other reasons were not wanting, he contended that the recent United States annexation of Texas was justified by the intrusion of foreign nations into this American matter "for the avowed object of thwarting our policy and hampering our power, limiting our greatness and checking the fulfillment of our manifest destiny to overspread the continent allotted by Providence for the

[1] Alexis de Tocqueville, *Democracy in America*, Phillips Bradley, ed. (New York, 1956), I, 450.

free development of our yearly multiplying millions." [2] Some years earlier another O'Sullivan essay in the *Democratic Review*, depicting America as "The Great Nation of Futurity," not only foreshadowed his use of the phrase manifest destiny, but also exemplified the transition from the peaceful idea of American mission to the aggressive concept of territorial expansion.

The far-reaching, the boundless future will be the era of American greatness. In its magnificent domain of space and time, the nation of many nations is destined to manifest to mankind the excellence of divine principles. . . . Its floor shall be the hemisphere—its roof the firmament of the star-studded heavens, and its congregation a Union of many Republics, comprising hundreds of happy millions, calling, owning no man master, but governed by God's natural and moral law of equality, the law of brotherhood—of "peace and good will amongst men." [3]

O'Sullivan's 1845 editorial reflected the view that Great Britain, by its continued occupation of Oregon and recognition of the Lone Star Republic of Texas, had interfered with American territorial progress. The Democratic party in 1844 had seemed to gauge correctly the strength of this American expansionist sentiment when it picked James K. Polk as its candidate and adopted a platform which included the resolution:

That our title to the whole of the Territory of Oregon is clear and unquestionable; that no portion of the same ought to be ceded to England or any other power, and that the re-occupation of Oregon and the re-annexation of Texas at the earliest and practicable period are great American measures, which this convention recommends to the cordial support of the Democracy of the Union. [4]

"These were the days," diplomatic historian Thomas A. Bailey has written, "when Manifest Destiny was a dynamic force—when it was widely believed that America's multiplying millions were manifestly destined to spread their republican institutions, though not necessarily by force, over at least the whole continent. These were the days when men talked of 'the universal Yankee nation' and 'an

[2] *United States Magazine and Democratic Review*, XVII (July–August, 1845), 5.

[3] *Ibid.*, VI (November, 1839), 427.

[4] *National Party Platforms, 1840–1960*, K. H. Porter and D. B. Johnson, eds. (Urbana, 1961), 4.

ocean-bound republic'; when the eagle was made to scream and the buffalo to bellow." [5]

Popular support for the notion of manifest destiny received tangible encouragement from a number of factors which, for the first time in American life, seemed to come together in the 1840's. Developing railroad lines and the experimental work in electricity which culminated in the Morse telegraph and promised better communication with the Far West overcame early American fears that the Pacific Coast could not be integrated with the rest of the nation. "The magnetic telegraph," the exuberant O'Sullivan wrote in 1845, "will enable the editors of the 'San Francisco Union,' the 'Astoria Evening Post,' or the 'Nootka Morning News' to set up in type the first half of the President's Inaugural before the echoes of the latter half shall have died away. . . ." [6] At the same time the belief that much of the plains and mountain area within the Louisiana Purchase—the so-called "Great American Desert"—was unsuited for agricultural settlement gave rise to an uneasy feeling that additional territories might be needed to satisfy the demands of land-hungry American pioneers and planters. Meanwhile the economic problems of the frontiersmen had been heightened by the hard times following the Panic of 1837. Texas and Oregon accordingly might offer a fresh start on the way to wealth. Finally, the prospect of bringing distant regions under the American flag had a jingoistic appeal for many citizens. A young and growing population, convinced of the reality of material progress, proved an eager audience for the expansionist propaganda of the penny press—the mass media of the new democracy. Andrew Jackson himself, the hero of this democracy, was an ardent expansionist who, in his own person and career, glamorized the spirit of manifest destiny.

Although the term manifest destiny proved a popular and useful phrase of justification and rationalization for the expansionist

    5 T. A. Bailey, *A Diplomatic History of the American People,* 3rd ed. (New York, 1947), 233–234.

    6 *United States Magazine and Democratic Review,* XVII (July–August, 1845), 9.

course of American foreign policy in the 1840's, the ideas and philosophy behind the words had wider ramifications. In the first place, manifest destiny conveyed a strong impression that American expansionism was inevitable and providential. Americans were a chosen people intended by Heaven to spread across the continent. Secondly, manifest destiny transformed such broad concepts as the idea of progress into the specific terms of a law of natural territorial growth. Third, it gave a new dynamic and positive value to the older doctrines of isolationism and the American mission. Neither isolationist nor missionary ideas were discarded. Instead, under the guiding hand of manifest destiny, they were imbued with greater nationalist vigor and precision. Thus the further accessions of territory in North America in the 1840's were viewed as strengthening the position of the United States and making its independence of Europe more certain. At the same time, the vague ideal of the American mission to spread democracy by example was translated into the actuality of the reach of free institutions across the continent.

In changing in this way the general into the specific, American foreign policy was, of course, also losing something of its idealistic and universal significance and appeal. While the concept of an American mission embraced a concern for the well-being of all nations and peoples, the doctrine of manifest destiny stressed the welfare of the United States. Moreover, despite the argument that expansion was the inevitable and inexorable fate decreed by Providence for the American people, there was actually a good deal of human will and effort which had to be called upon before the goals of manifest destiny could be reached. For example, much political agitation and propaganda, war, and threat of war, had to take place before the territorial aspirations of the advocates of manifest destiny were achieved.

Manifest destiny was an expression of exaggerated nationalism in American foreign policy. This expansionism of the 1840's was nationalist, not in the sense that it enjoyed the united support of all Americans, but in the way in which the nation selfishly pursued its own interests at the expense of other nations. While isolationism and the concept of an American mission were, of course, also nationalistic, neither concept was as aggressive as that of manifest destiny. Isolationism stressed the defense and security of the American

Republic in a world of hostile European monarchies. And the idea of mission, though expansionist, emphasized on the whole the peaceful export of American ideology and the realization of the natural rights of man through the spread of American political institutions. In contrast, the concept of manifest destiny implied expansion in a more belligerent manner. It turned the defensive and idealistic notions of isolationism and mission toward the course of a unilateral, nationalist, political and territorial expansion. And, in so doing it also transposed broader, more universal values of genuine international importance—the natural rights philosophy, for example—into a narrower doctrine of the special rights of Americans over and against other peoples.

In pursuit of its goals the United States had the immense advantage of being able to work out its destiny without the serious opposition of other world powers. At the very birth of American expansionist designs in the first years of the Republic, Europe was absorbed in the French Revolutionary and Napoleonic struggles. Thus American foreign policy was able to profit immediately from the strife of Europe. As J. Fred Rippy points out, not only is it "doubtful indeed whether the United States would even have been born," but "A harmonious Europe would never have permitted the United States to extend its boundaries and its political dominance from the Appalachians to the Pacific Ocean and from the tropical Caribbean to the snows of Alaska." [7]

Finally, it should be noted that the doctrine of manifest destiny not only implied inevitability, but it also indicated that the process of expansion was unlimited in time or place. Once the Pacific Coast had been reached, Americans looked outward across the waters to the islands and shores beyond. And then, as the desire for new territories and overseas dependencies eventually waned, manifest destiny was increasingly identified with the search for foreign markets and the desire to exercise a dominating military and ideological influence in world affairs. Thus the general philosophy and outlook of manifest destiny became one of the major controlling assumptions underlying American foreign policy in both the nineteenth and twentieth centuries.

In the course of the contemporary justification of manifest des-

[7] J. F. Rippy, *America and the Strife of Europe* (Chicago, 1938), 103.

tiny as distinct from the more material factors which also influenced expansionism, the American people invoked, as Albert K. Weinberg's massive scholarly study of nationalist expansion has shown, a wealth of argument and illustration, touching virtually every aspect of American foreign policy. From the natural rights philosophy of the American Revolution to the assertions of world leadership in the twentieth century, American spokesmen described at length what they understood to be the destined direction of United States expansion. Except briefly in the crisis of the Civil War, American confidence in the manifest destiny of the nation hardly wavered. For, in the words of Franklin Roosevelt, the American people quite literally always believed that they had a rendezvous with destiny.

Long before the phrase manifest destiny was coined to describe the nationalist expansion of the United States, the philosophy implicit in the term had already begun to affect the foreign policy of the new nation. The natural rights argument, which bulked so large in the contentions of the Revolutionary patriots, was accordingly put to use to justify American territorial expansion beyond the confines of the thirteen Colonies or States. Thus the Revolutionary natural rights to freedom from taxation without representation and to national self-determination were broadened to include the natural right to security and self-preservation through the extension of American territory. On this basis, Americans in 1776 launched an invasion of Canada and contended that the acquisition of Florida and Nova Scotia might also become necessary measures of self-defense.

Although the United States secured generally acceptable boundaries by the Peace Treaty of 1783, the Mississippi River proved an unsatisfactory western limit because the Spanish Empire controlled its mouth at New Orleans. Americans claimed henceforth that free navigation of the river was their natural right, and in behalf of his Congressional resolution affirming this belief Senator James Ross told his colleagues that "so important a right would never be secure, while the mouth of the Mississippi was exclusively in the hands of the Spaniards."[8] According to the Boston clergyman Jedidiah Morse, better known as the author of the first American geography and history textbooks, "the Mississippi was never designed as the western boundary of the American empire. The God of nature never intended that some of the best part of his earth should be inhabited by the subjects of a monarch, 4,000 miles from them." Confident that "when the rights of mankind shall be more fully known," the power of the European monarchs would be confined to the Old World, Morse predicted "the period, as not far distant, when the AMERICAN EMPIRE will comprehend millions of souls west of the Mississippi."[9]

The purchase of Louisiana, an application of Jefferson's agricultural imperialism, gained for the United States not only the possession of the much-coveted mouth of the Mississippi but also the lands to the west as far as the Rocky Mountains. At first American thought, personified by Jefferson and Thomas Hart Benton, inclined to the view that the Rockies should form a natural limit to further United States political expansion. Although Jefferson envisaged other New World republics, peopled by the sons and daughters of the United States, he did not believe that the American flag and Constitution could be extended to regions far beyond the range of reasonable travel and communication. The United States might be a "nest" from which other American republics would emerge in time,[10] but the Jeffersonians were not interested in statemaking beyond the Rockies. Even as late as 1836, Horace Greeley, the Whig editor, in his opposition to further American expansion "would have been content to see our western limits fixed at the Rocky Mountains."[11]

On the whole, however, the accession of the Louisiana territory, almost doubling the extent of the United States, did little to still the demands for further expansion. Florida, which had long been linked in the American mind with New Orleans, was now regarded as an

[8] February 14, 1803, *Annals of Congress*, 7, Cong., 2 Sess., 86.

[9] Jedidiah Morse, *The American Geography* (Elizabethtown, 1789), 469.

[10] *Papers of Thomas Jefferson*, J. P. Boyd, ed. (Princeton, 1950–   ), IX, 218.

[11] G. C. Van Deusen, "The Nationalism of Horace Greeley," in *Nationalism and Internationalism*, E. M. Earle, ed. (New York, 1950), 435.

even more necessary acquisition if the United States was to reach its natural boundaries. "God and nature have destined New Orleans and the Floridas to belong to this great and rising empire," was the judgment pronounced by Andrew Jackson while he was serving in the United States Senate.[12] In contrast to the situation of Spain in faraway Europe, the United States by virtue of its territorial propinquity was viewed as having superior natural claims to the Florida and Texas territories, both of which, it was argued, should have been included in the Louisiana Purchase.

By the Adams-Onís Treaty of 1819 which gained Florida, the United States yielded its claims to Texas and took over the Spanish claims to the Oregon country. For the next two decades direct American interest in the Far West was confined to a scattering of adventuresome explorers and traders. Gradually, however, under the growing conviction that it was the geographical predestination of the United States to carry its flag from the Atlantic to the Pacific Ocean, even such a seemingly formidable natural barrier as the Rocky Mountains was dismissed as inconsequential. As early as 1823 Representative Francis Baylies, in contrast to the more conservative views of most of his colleagues, predicted:

If we reach the Rocky Mountains, we should be unwise did we not pass that narrow space which separates the mountains from the ocean, to secure advantages far greater than the existing advantages of all the country between the Mississippi and the mountains. Gentlemen are talking of natural boundaries. Sir. our natural boundary is the Pacific Ocean. The swelling tide of our population must and will roll on until that mighty ocean interposes its waters, and limits our territorial empire.[13]

While the Rockies served as no insurmountable geographic obstacle to American claims to Oregon, to the Southwest it was argued that the United States should have the water boundary of the Rio Grande as a natural frontier. Texas, according to Thomas Hart Benton, Robert J. Walker, and other expansionists, was a part of the natural Mississippi River basin, and as such should never have been yielded by the United States in 1819. Seemingly, when the rights of other nations to natural boundaries conflicted with the

[12] February 23, 1803, *Annals of Congress,* 7 Cong., 2 Sess., 150.
[13] January 24, 1823, *ibid.,* 17 Cong., 2 Sess., 682–683.

similar aspirations of the American people, the United States, according to the expansionist argument, had a special right and destiny.

Although the Spanish and British empires had claims to certain disputed North American territories which antedated those of the United States, in a true sense all such claims were derived originally from the Indians' possession of the soil. For the red man as for the Europeans, however, a most important American contention was that neither had any real rights to land that was needed by American settlers. In American eyes the progress of civilization required that the greater part of the North American Continent, including even those territories not yet under the United States flag, be put to its highest and best use. The Indians had the right only to such lands as they were able to occupy and cultivate. Already in 1633 the General Court in Massachusetts decreed that "what lands any of the Indians have possessed and improved, by subduing the same, they have just right unto." But what this meant primarily was indicated by Governor Winthrop who pointed out that "the Indians having only a natural right to so much land as they had or could improve . . . the rest of the country lay open to any that could and would improve it." [14]

Humanitarian objections to the dispossession of the Indian from his ancestral lands were therefore largely brushed aside, and American sympathy with the red man became effective only when the Indians had no further territory to lose. Otherwise, the occupation of the land was for white men. In the words of Senator Benton: "The white race were a land-loving people, and had a right to possess it because they used it according to the intentions of the CREATOR." [15] "Is one of the fairest portions of the globe to remain in the state of nature, the haunt of a few wretched savages," asked William Henry Harrison, Governor of Indiana Territory, "when it seems destined by the Creator to give support to a large population

14 Quoted in A. K. Weinberg, *Manifest Destiny* (Baltimore, 1935), 75.
15 January 12, 1843, *Congressional Globe*, 27 Cong., 3 Sess., Appendix, 74.

and to be the seat of civilization, of science, and of true religion?" [16]

A widely held American opinion was that the Indians were doomed to yield their territory to the white man because of their own lack of progress in the arts of civilization. The Pennsylvania frontier writer Hugh Henry Brackenridge was perhaps hardly exaggerating popular American views when he wrote in 1782 that "extermination" should be the fate for "the animals vulgarly called Indians for not having made "a better use of the land." [17] But in the case of the Cherokee and other civilized tribes in the area of Georgia's western lands, their problem was precisely a result of the fact that they had adopted successfully the white man's ways, making their lands more valuable and desirable in the process. As Calhoun observed in a cabinet meeting in 1824, the whole difficulty with the Cherokees stemmed from their progress in civilization.[18]

In a technical sense United States relations with the various Indian tribes were governed by the treaty-making process. In this way the Indians yielded title to most of their lands east of the Mississippi. These treaties, however, received scant respect from most American politicians, except as they opened the way for westward expansion. According to Governor George R. Gilmer of Georgia:

> Treaties were expedients by which ignorant, intractable, and savage people were induced without bloodshed to yield up what civilized peoples had a right to possess by virtue of that command of the Creator delivered to man upon his formation—be fruitful, multiply, and replenish the earth, and subdue it.[19]

The Indians obviously were at best dependent nations, and the unilateral policy of the United States was clearly one of removing the tribes beyond the encroaching frontiers of settlement. Jefferson while President encouraged the Cherokees to accept new lands beyond the Mississippi, and Congress gave such a program definite authorization by the Indian Removal Act of 1830. President Jackson, despite the famous interposition of the Supreme Court in the Georgia Cherokee cases, moved quickly to see that the Con-

---

[16] Quoted in Weinberg, *Manifest Destiny*, 79.

[17] Quoted in *ibid.*, 77.

[18] *Memoirs of John Quincy Adams*, C. F. Adams, ed. (Philadelphia, 1874–1877), VI, 272.

[19] Quoted in Weinberg, *Manifest Destiny*, 83.

gressional intentions were carried out. "Professing a desire to civilize and settle" the Indians, the United States Government, Jackson admitted, "at the same time lost no opportunity to purchase their lands and thrust them farther into the wilderness." Personally convinced that the prospect of the Indians' civilization was hopeless and that their territory belonged to the land-hungry Americans, Jackson declared that the removal policy of the Administration "will place a dense and civilized population in large tracts of country now occupied by a few savage hunters." In summing up his views, Jackson told Congress in 1835:

> The plan of removing the aboriginal people who yet remain within the settled portions of the United States to the country west of the Mississippi River approaches its consummation. It was adopted on the most mature consideration of the condition of this race, and ought to be persisted in till the object is accomplished, and prosecuted with as much vigor as a just regard to their circumstances will permit, and as fast as their consent can be obtained. All preceding experiments for the improvement of the Indians have failed. It seems now to be an established fact that they cannot live in contact with a civilized community and prosper.[20]

Until after the Civil War the Indians were able to find a haven in the lands between the Mississippi Valley and the Rocky Mountains. But this plains and desert area was only a temporary refuge, and the Indians were gradually forced to accept confinement upon the specific reservations allotted for their use. At the same time Congress, recognizing reality, substituted American law and administrative authority for the largely fictitious policy of dealing with the tribes as foreign nations. The Indians henceforth were a factor in American foreign policy only as their historic fate inspired criticisms from abroad of the methods of American expansionism.

Increasingly in the 1840's arguments used to justify the progress of manifest destiny in relation to the Indians proved useful as well to support American policies with respect to Mexico and Oregon.

20 *A Compilation of the Messages and Papers of the Presidents, 1789–1897*, J. D. Richardson, ed. (Washington, 1896–1899), III, 171.

At the expense of the Indian tribes the national domain of the United States was gradually being increased without the addition of new foreign territories, but merely through the acts and treaties by which the Indians' land claims were extinguished. Louisiana and Florida had also been acquired by treaty, but in the mid-forties the workings of American diplomacy no longer seemed so inexorable or automatic. Mexico refused to recognize the annexation of Texas, and Great Britain continued to be reluctant to yield all of Oregon. At this juncture, as the Polk Administration called upon the country to prepare for war to defend what was regarded as its true title to both Oregon and Texas, American expansionists invoked the higher sanction of an appeal to democracy. Possession of Texas and Oregon, it was said, would extend the area of freedom and further the progress of civilization.

This incantation to democracy to justify American acquisition of Texas and Oregon was a relatively new form of the expansionist argument. Jefferson, it is true, had referred to the idea of "an empire for liberty" to include Canada, Florida, and even Cuba, but democracy as a positive ideal was seldom used to support the case for American territorial expansion until the 1830's and '40's. Although Jefferson expressed the view that possession of an extensive territory would strengthen American democracy by minimizing the divisive force of selfish local interests, he also shared the widespread feeling that the growth of free institutions could be achieved best by peaceful example rather than through force. Thus there seemed to be a distinction in the American mind between the general mission to advance democracy and free institutions and the specific desire to annex new lands.

The extension of democracy had not been an important factor in the early American expansionist interest in Louisiana or Florida. And, in the case of the inhabitants of New Orleans, the United States had acted tardily in enabling them to benefit from the American practice of local self-government. But the opinion of many of the Revolutionary and Founding Fathers that a republican form of government and free institutions could not well be extended over large areas was gradually weakened as the United States gained new territories and indulged in expansionist dreams in the War of 1812. "The expansion of our Union over a vast territory can not operate unfavorably to the States individually," President Monroe declared in 1822. "With governments separate, vigorous, and efficient for all local purposes, their distance from each other can have no injurious effect upon their respective interests." [21] By the 1830's all remaining American apprehensions of this incompatibility of democracy and territorial growth virtually disappeared in the midst of the strong desires of the country to gain Canada, Cuba, Texas, Oregon, and California.

Important additional support for the linkage of democracy and expansion was provided by American concern over European ambitions in North America. As Professor Rippy has remarked, "manifest destiny never pointed to the acquisition of a region so unmistakably as when undemocratic, conservative Europe revealed an inclination to interfere or to absorb." [22] Although the Texas Republic already enjoyed political freedom, British commercial interests there encouraged American expansionists to call for annexation in order to preserve democracy. Some Texans, it is true, resented such a patronizing attitude on the part of their fellow Americans to the north, and abolitionists and antiexpansionists also complained vigorously that the United States wished to extend the area of freedom by enlarging the area of slavery. Once the Texas question became a part of war with Mexico, however, expansionists were able to contend that the boundaries of political freedom were being extended over regions hitherto suffering from Mexican misrule.

In the course of the Mexican War, United States interest in carrying the benefits of democracy south of the Rio Grande became intertwined with the contention that the war was necessary as a part of an American mission of regeneration for the Mexican people. Under the spell of the idea that the Anglo-Saxon countries were destined to conquer the world, American nativists considered the Mexicans an inferior people. While some expansionists, desiring only territory, warned that the United States would be corrupted by intimate contact with a non-Anglo-Saxon race, others were eager to accept responsibility for the regeneration of so-called lesser nationalities. When the results of the war left American armies of occupation

21 *Ibid.*, II, 177.
22 J. F. Rippy, *The United States and Mexico* (New York, 1926), 29.

in command of large areas of Mexican territory, the editors of prominent Democratic publications were quick to accept the mission of regeneration for the United States. "The latter expectation," Weinberg comments, "perhaps showed more optimism than the previous history of military occupations warranted." But the enthusiasm of the *New York Herald*, at least, was undaunted:

> The uinversal Yankee nation can regenerate and disenthrall the people of Mexico in a few years; and we believe it is a part of our destiny to civilize that beautiful country and enable its inhabitants to appreciate some of the many advantages and blessings they enjoy.[23]

As the appetite for expansion grew with the war, some Americans came around to the view that even all of Mexico might safely be absorbed by the United States. The *Democratic Review*, which had previously opposed such complete annexation, now declared in February, 1848:

> Whatever danger there may be in blending people of different religions into one nation, where religion is established by law,—or in annexing by conquest, under arbitrary governments, which trample upon the rights of all their subjects, and conquer only to enslave,—a free nation, which shows equal toleration and protection to all religions, and conquers only to bestow freedom, has no such danger to fear.[24]

In their acceptance of an American destiny to regenerate the Mexican people and extend the benefits of freedom to their Government, the expansionists of the 1840's were anticipating the argument, fifty years later, of the white man's burden. Meanwhile, in the midst of nativist hostility to European immigrants, the doctrine of an Anglo-Saxon civilizing mission to all lesser races became in a sense the positive aspect of American pride and prejudice. As the national feelings toward the Indians and Mexicans demonstrated, an egocentric and ethnocentric intolerance was becoming an important part of the philosophy of manifest destiny. In the 1840's and 50's the rationale of manifest destiny in all of its varied ramifications gave vital backing to the aggressive goals of American foreign policy. And, at the same time, the angry protests of those who op-

23 *New York Herald*, May 15, 1847, in Weinberg, *Manifest Destiny*, 171.

24 *United States Magazine and Democratic Review*, XXII (February, 1848), 119–120.

posed this expansionism were effectively countered by the claim that
American arms and diplomacy carried in their wake the blessings
of democracy and civilization.

In Oregon the pressure of the pioneers taking the westward trail
in the 1840's made untenable joint occupation of the territory with
Great Britain. The farmers of the Northwest associated an expanding frontier with American individualism and economic opportunity. Oregon, it was said, "must be occupied for poor men who
needed homes and for the extension of free institutions," and this
economic individualism "perhaps did more than anything to cement
the association between democracy and expansion." [25] To the
pioneers democracy meant economic opportunity as well as a form
of government. British fur trading interests in the Northwest as
well as British monarchy were, therefore, a threat to American
democratic expansionism. While England wanted to keep Oregon
"for the benefit of the wild beasts as well as of the savage nations,"
John Quincy Adams, in upholding the American claims to 54° 40',
asserted that the national purpose was "To make the wilderness
blossom as the rose, to establish laws, to increase, multiply, and subdue the earth. . . ." [26]

In his denunciation of British imperialism in Oregon, Senator
William Allen of Ohio declared that exclusive American occupation
would give the United States "the first place in the modern system of
the world, . . . leading it on to that social regeneration, which
promises the delivery of mankind from the miseries of antiquated
monarchy." [27] "Expansionism, later to be depicted by anti-imperialists as a means to economic exploitation and slavery, was seen in
this period as a means to economic liberty. Economic freedom had
become as important as political freedom to the philosophy of democracy. . . . Freedom for the American nation; freedom for the

25 H. C. Hubbart, "Regionalism and Democracy in the Middle West," in
Democracy in the Middle West, J. P. Nichols and J. G. Randall, eds. (New
York, 1941), 66; Weinberg, *Manifest Destiny*, 116.

26 February 9, 1846, *Congressional Globe*, 29 Cong., 1 Sess., 342.

27 February 10–11, 1846, *ibid.*, 29 Cong., 1 Sess., Appendix, 839.

American State; freedom for the American individual; such then were the principal elements in the fundamentally egoistic program of extending the area of freedom." [28]

The extravagant hopes of the American pioneer in the West were illustrated in the career of a young soldier and journalist, William Gilpin. Gilpin was a personal friend of Andrew Jackson, who appointed him to West Point. Later he came into contact with such ardent Western expansionists as Thomas Hart Benton and John Charles Frémont. Returning to Washington in 1844 from an expedition to the Oregon country with Frémont, Gilpin found employment as an expert adviser to Benton, Buchanan, Polk, and other expansionist-minded Democratic statesmen. Then, after Army service in the Mexican War and a later stint of fighting against the Pawnees and Commanches, Gilpin turned to writing and speaking about the West. In one of the first examples of his literary work Gilpin summed up in grandiloquent fashion the millenium that he foresaw if the workings of manifest destiny were fulfilled:

The *untransacted* destiny of the American people is to subdue the continent—to rush over this vast field to the Pacific Ocean—to animate the many hundred millions of its people, and to cheer them upward . . . —to agitate these herculean masses—to establish a new order in human affairs . . . —to regenerate superannuated nations— . . . to stir up the sleep of a hundred centuries—to teach old nations a new civilization—to confirm the destiny of the human race—to carry the career of mankind to its culminating point—to cause a stagnant people to be reborn—to perfect science—to emblazon history with the conquest of peace—to shed a new and resplendent glory upon mankind—to unite the world in one social family—to dissolve the spell of tyranny and exalt charity—to absolve the curse that weighs down humanity, and to shed blessings round the world! [29]

In language as extravagant as Gilpin's, James D. B. De Bow, the New Orleans magazine editor, in the journal that bore his name, exclaimed in 1850:

We have a destiny to perform, a 'manifest destiny' over all Mexico, over South America, over the West Indies and Canada. The Sandwich Islands are as necessary to our eastern, as the isles of the gulf to our western commerce. The gates of the Chinese empire must be thrown down

28 Weinberg, *Manifest Destiny,* 116, 121–122.
29 Quoted in H. N. Smith, *Virgin Land* (Cambridge, Mass., 1950), 37.

by the men from the Sacramento and the Oregon, and the haughty Japanese tramplers upon the cross be enlightened in the doctrines of republicanism and the ballot box. The eagle of the republic shall poise itself over the field of Waterloo, after tracing its flight among the gorges of the Himalaya or the Ural mountains, and a successor of Washington ascend the chair of universal empire! These are the giddy dreams of the day. The martial spirit must have its employ. The people stand ready to hail tomorrow, with shouts and enthusiasm, a collision with the proudest and the mightiest empire on earth.[30]

The territorial growth which Americans proudly rationalized in the extraordinarily elastic meanings that they assigned to the concept of manifest destiny had been accomplished with an abnormal amount of speed in the 1840's. But the winning of Texas, Oregon, and California for the American flag did not curtail the activities of American expansionists. The success of the Mexican War, instead of satiating, merely whetted their appetite for more territory. Even though the regions already acquired seemed to be in excess of any immediate national needs, Southern slaveholders, for example, were far from satisfied. Thus the early 1850's saw the climax of American efforts to annex Cuba and other lands deemed suitable for the extension of slavery.

That the sole expansionist achievement of the 1850's was the purchase of a strip of southwest territory by Gadsden's Treaty was, it has been suggested, more a matter of lack of luck than of boldness. President Pierce, as a representative of the "Young America" expansionist wing of the Democratic party, frankly favored an aggressive foreign policy. In his Inaugural Address he announced that the policies of his administration would "not be controlled by any timid forebodings of evil from expansion. . . . The apprehension of dangers from extended territory, multiplied States, accumulated wealth, and augmented population has proved to be unfounded," he declared.[31] Pierce accordingly gave his support to the Perry ex-

---

[30] DeBow's Southern and Western Review, IX (August, 1850), 167–168.
[31] Messages and Papers of the Presidents, V, 198.

pedition to Japan, initiated by his Whig predecessor, and only the renewed sectional dispute over slavery following the Kansas-Nebraska bill forestalled more ambitious expansionist projects in Cuba and the Caribbean. By antagonizing antislavery opinion the Kansas-Nebraska bill insured the opposition of the North to the longstanding American hopes of acquiring the island of Cuba, and the Pierce administration had to admit the defeat of its expansionist dreams.

Although prospects for territorial growth in specific areas were therefore dim by the mid-fifties, the overall confidence of the advocates of manifest destiny was hardly diminished. "Expansion," said President Buchanan, "is in the future the policy of our country, and only cowards fear and oppose it." [32] Whatever their temporary disappointments, American expansionists could take refuge in their unassailable confidence that growth was the law of nature for all healthy nations. The historic extension of American territory and the ever-increasing American population were assurances that this natural growth was indeed the destined future of the Republic. To themselves, Americans felt, the famous observation of Humboldt was applied with particular force: "It is with nations as with nature which knows no pause in progress and development, and attaches her curse on all inaction." [33]

Even those who drew back from the more extreme notions of manifest destiny were content to accept the accessions that might be expected to come from the natural growth of the American national domain. Thus Edward Everett, the scholarly Secretary of State in the anti-expansionist Fillmore Administration, in countering an Anglo-French proposal to tie American hands in regard to Cuba, adroitly suggested that in contrast to the foreign policies of the Old World, that of the United States was subject to "the law of American growth and progress." [34] Like Everett a man of peace, Parke Godwin, in his book of political essays published in 1854, wrote:

Precisely, however, because this tendency to the assimilation of foreign ingredients, or the putting forth of new members, is an inevitable in-

[32] Quoted in J. M. Callahan, *Cuba and International Relations* (Baltimore, 1899), 304–305.

[33] Quoted in W. W. Greenough, *The Conquering Republic* (Boston, 1849), 34.

[34] J. B. Moore, *A Digest of International Law* (Washington, 1906), VI, 469.

cident of our growth . . . there is no need that it should be especially
fostered or stimulated. It will thrive of itself; it will supply the fuel of its
own fires; and all that it requires is only a wise direction. . . . The fruit
will fall into our hands when it is ripe, without an officious shaking of the
tree. Cuba will be ours, and Canada and Mexico, too—if we want them—
in due season, and without the wicked imperative of a war.[35]

Less forbearing and patient than Everett or Godwin, the Democratic expansionists of the late 1850's were continually hopeful that
this law of natural growth and expansion would once again receive
official political encouragement. Southern annexationists and their
supporters, in particular, refused to concede that the Kansas-
Nebraska question had doomed all chance for the acquisition of
Cuba and other potential slave territory. Sympathetic with these
expectations and convinced that Mexico, and perhaps Cuba, lay
within the path of American destiny, Caleb Cushing asked:

Is not the occupation of any portion of the earth by those competent
to hold and till it, a providential law of national life? Can you say to the
tide that it ought not to flow, or the rain to fall? I reply, *it must!* And so
it is with well-constituted, and therefore, progressive and expansive nations.
They cannot help advancing; it is the condition of their existence.[36]

A Senate report, advocating the purchase of Cuba in 1859, declared:
"The law of our national existence is growth. We cannot, if we
would disobey it. While we should do nothing to stimulate it unnaturally, we should be careful not to impose upon ourselves a
regimen so strict as to prevent its healthful development." [37] And on
the eve of the Civil War, retired Congressman J. F. H. Claiborne, in
defending the American filibusters who sought to liberate Cuba,
asserted:

We proceed upon the theory that the condition of a republic is repose.
What an error! That is the normal condition of absolutism. The law of
a republic is progress. Its nature is aggressive.

We are in the restless period of youth; the law of the age is progress;
let our flag be given to the winds, and our principles go with it wherever

35 Parke Godwin, *Political Essays* (New York, 1856), 169.
36 Quoted in C. M. Fuess, *The Life of Caleb Cushing* (New York, 1923),
II, 225.
37 Quoted in Weinberg, *Manifest Destiny*, 202.

it is unfurled. Conquest is essential to our internal repose. War sometimes becomes the best security for peace.[38]

Not only was natural growth the manifest destiny of the American nation, but the attempt to violate this law could be the harbinger of disaster. The nations that failed to advance with the progress of civilization could not expect to enjoy the repose of stability. Instead, the alternative to progress was swift descent in a retrograde motion. In making out his case for the accession of Cuba, a writer in the *Democratic Review* for 1859 observed:

'We are governed by the laws under which the universe was created;' and therefore, in obedience to those laws, we must of necessity move forward in the paths of destiny shaped for us by the great Ruler of the Universe. Activity and progress is the law of heaven and of earth; and in the 'violation of this law there is danger.'[39]

This same thought in connection with expansionist ambitions was expressed earlier by the magazine writers who pointed out:

Civilization is a progressive work—there is no standing still—its principle is continual advancement. The nation that ceases to go forward must certainly go back.

National glory—national greatness—the spread of political liberty on this continent, must be the thought and action by day, and the throbbing dream by night, of the whole American people, or they will sink into oblivion.[40]

Thus the advocates of manifest destiny found support for their ambitious views in the philosophical concept of the idea of progress. The law of progress for nations, as for individuals, indicated growth and activity as the only alternative to decline and death.

As the Civil War cast its shadow over the land to disrupt the course of American manifest destiny, American expansionists were forced to postpone their conviction that Cuba, Canada, Mexico, and other regions in the New World would eventually come under the American flag. But confidence in the force of American political gravitation and in the inevitability of the American destiny was not

[38] J. F. H. Claibourne, *Life and Correspondence of John A. Quitman* (New York, 1860), II, 111, 113.

[39] *United States' Democratic Review*, XLIII (April, 1859), 32.

[40] *Scientific American*, II (July 31, 1847), 357; *New York Herald*, October 11, 1852, in Weinberg, *Manifest Destiny*, 207.

lost. While the Civil War armies were joined in their fearful struggle, Darwinian concepts of evolution and competition emerged to provide new arguments for growth, and to create a bridge from the manifest destiny of the early nineteenth century to the imperialism of later years. At the same time the achievement of a stronger national union as a result of the Civil War reinforced American security and helped to establish thereby the foundations for the development of the United States as a major world power.

SELECTED REFERENCES

Darling, Arthur B. *Our Rising Empire, 1763–1803*. New Haven: Yale University Press, 1940.

Graebner, Norman A. *Empire on the Pacific: A Study in American Continental Expansion*. New York: Ronald Press, 1955.

Merk, Frederick. *Manifest Destiny and Mission in American History*. New York: Knopf, 1963.

Nichols, J. P. and James G. Randall, eds. *Democracy in the Middle West, 1840–1940*. New York: Appleton-Century, 1941.

Parish, John C. *The Emergence of the Idea of Manifest Destiny*. Los Angeles: University of California Press, 1932.

Smith Henry Nash. *Virgin Land: The American West as Symbol and Myth*. Cambridge, Mass.: Harvard University Press. 1950.

Van Alstyne, R. W. *The Rising American Empire*. New York: Oxford University Press, 1960.

Weinberg, Albert K. *Manifest Destiny: A Study of Nationalist Expansionism in American History*. Baltimore: Johns Hopkins Press, 1935.

IV

A Stronger National Union

The independence of the United States was never really in doubt after the War of 1812, but it was not until a half-century later that the national unity of the country was assured. "It took the United States a long time to consolidate as a nation," a leading historian of American nationalism has written. "This is not astonishing," he adds, in view of the fact that "the area which it covered was a continent rather than a country."[1] The federal system, it is true, provided an answer for those who feared that the bonds of union could not be stretched to cover an enlarged territory. But even this political innovation could not overcome the strong sectional feelings of the country. Well before the South carried out its long-threatened secession in 1861, the Federal union had already been menaced by early separatist sentiment in the West and in New England. And only after the Civil War—the most bitter and bloody conflict in all the Western world in the century between 1815 and 1914—did the United States become a truly unified and national state.

If the ultimate effect of the territorial growth of the United States before the Civil War was to strengthen American nationalism, the more immediate fruits of this manifest destiny were the weakening and disruption of the Federal union. Expansion westward, despite its promise for the future, brought to a climax the increasing antagonism of the North and South over slavery. This division was part of a sectionalism which extended even into the area of foreign policy. Southern Congressmen, for example, were reluctant to vote the larger naval appropriations needed for efficient United States

[1] Hans Kohn, *American Nationalism* (New York, 1957), 93.

cooperation in the international effort to stamp out the African slave trade. The North, in turn, in its opposition to augmenting the potential area of slavery, withdrew its backing from the old American dream of annexing Cuba. In the Pacific as well as in the Caribbean in the 1850's, the renewal of the slavery controversy following the Kansas-Nebraska Act foreclosed the expansionist designs of American diplomacy. Both the North and the South were unable any longer to agree on the proper course for American foreign policy, and sectional division accordingly became as much a part of external as of internal affairs in the decade before the Civil War.

The waxing domestic discord over slavery could not but weaken the position of the United States in the eyes of the rest of the world. Although of all countries the United States was probably the best situated to undergo such an experience, historically civil wars had ever served as invitations to foreign interference or intervention. Even though this might have seemed a remote contingency before 1861, a number of European governments, in their resentment over American expansionism, were not unwilling to abet the disruption of the Federal union. So long as America stood divided by slavery and civil war, neither its republican institutions nor its growing population and territory offered any serious challenge to the monarchies of the Old World. Both the idea of an American political mission and the concept of manifest destiny were, for the time being at least, effectively forestalled.

Almost thirty years before the Civil War came, at a time when South Carolina's nullification of the Tariff of 1832 created one of the first of the major sectional crises in the United States, Joel R. Poinsett, a Southern Unionist, brought the people of his state a message from the revered hero of the American Revolution, the Marquis de Lafayette. "Tell your countrymen," the venerable French patriot confided to Poinsett "that if they are so mad and so wicked as to quarrel among themselves about the mere matter of interest, about five or six per cent more or less for duties, . . . they will discredit republican government throughout the world. . . . We are looking anxiously to them, for if they are so blind as to dissolve the Union, and cause the failure of the great experiment . . . , we who are contending for freedom on this side of the Atlantic must lie down in despair and die in our chains." [2]

2 J. F. Rippy, *America and the Strife of Europe* (Chicago, 1938), 32.

Lafayette's appeal to American unity and to the historic force of the American example stated a theme which was echoed by Andrew Jackson in his messages to Congress discussing the nullification issue. On such an occasion, "so interesting and important in our history, and of such anxious concern to the friends of freedom throughout the world," the President urged that selfish and local considerations be laid aside in favor of a return to the principles of a government of laws and of a Federal union based on popular representation. "After a successful experiment of forty-four years, at a moment when the Government and the Union are the objects of the hopes of friends of civil liberty throughout the world," Jackson noted that the American people were being called upon to decide "whether these laws possess any force and that Union the means of self-preservation." [3]

In the midst of the Civil War, this feeling that the fate of free institutions everywhere would be affected by the disruption of the American Union continued to be a popular belief both at home and abroad. Lincoln gave such a view its classic expression in his Gettysburg Address, in which he depicted the United States as "engaged in a great civil war, testing whether that nation, or any nation so conceived and so dedicated, can long endure." Earlier, in his message to a special session of Congress, he had raised the question of whether there was some inherent fatal weakness in republics which made them either too strong for the liberties of their own people or too weak to maintain their existence. But, in respect to the significance of the Civil War abroad, Lincoln was well aware that "Our struggle has been, of course, contemplated by foreign nations with reference less to its own merits than its supposed and exaggerated effects and consequences resulting to those nations themselves." [4]

Among the interested observers of the American Civil War in Europe there were perhaps as many partisans of the South as of the

[3] *A Compilation of the Messages and Papers of the Presidents, 1789–1897,* J. D. Richardson, ed. (Washington, 1896–1899), II, 605–606, 631.

[4] *Ibid.,* VI, 126–127.

North. To some it seemed that the Southern states, by fighting for their self-determination as a nation, were striking a blow for political freedom and independence in the spirit of similar revolutionary national movements in the Old World. Southerners themselves contended that they were following the example of the American Patriots of 1776—a point of view which appeared reasonable to many Englishmen. According to the London *Times:*

> The contest is really for empire on the side of the North, and for independence on that of the South, and in this respect we recognize an exact analogy between the North and the Government of George III, and the South and the Thirteen Revolted Provinces. These opinions may be wrong, but they are the general opinions of the English nation. . . .[5]

Conservatives abroad now were able to rejoice that a republic was no more immune to violence and revolution than a monarchy. To the British aristocracy it appeared clear that, while a victory for the North would encourage the disfranchised masses in England to clamor more loudly than ever for democracy, a defeat for the Union would discredit democratic tendencies abroad. Divided, the United States would not be so formidable a rival nor such a menace to Canada and other British possessions in North America. The Old World again would have an opportunity to assert its influence in the New. In England, after a series of Northern defeats on the battlefield, the London *Times* reported that "people are breathing more freely, and talking more lightly of the United States, than they have done any time these thirty years." But if the North was able eventually to prevail, the London *Morning Post* told its readers that "Democracy will be more arrogant, more aggressive, more levelling and vulgarizing, if that is possible, than it ever had been before." [6]

In English liberal circles, and among the friends of the North, there was the hope that a war fought for the expressed purpose of restoring the Union, would also result in the freeing of the slaves. Despite the American eagerness to serve as an example of democracy, English liberals could not overlook the fact that by 1860, in all the

[5] London *Times*, November 7, 1861, in T. A. Bailey, *A Diplomatic History of the American People*, 7th ed. (New York, 1964), 320.

[6] London *Times*, August 15, 1862, in *ibid.*, 321–322; London *Morning Post*, February 22, 1862, in E. D. Adams, *Great Britain and the American Civil War* (London, 1925), II, 284.

civilized portions of the globe, slavery continued only in the United States, Brazil, Cuba, and Puerto Rico. In defending the cause of the American Union in the court of world opinion, therefore, it was this concentration of slavery in the South, in contrast to the growing prospect for emancipation if the North won the war, which ultimately furnished Lincoln with a decisive diplomatic weapon with which to gain European sympathies—of the masses if not of the governments.

Despite some spectacular successes scored by the Confederate diplomats early in the war and despite the economic importance of the South's cotton, the North on the whole was able to manage its foreign affairs satisfactorily. In general, the chief threat to traditional American interests in foreign policy which occurred during the war years was in connection with the Monroe Doctrine. Both Spain and France took some advantage of the preoccupation of the North and South to intervene directly in Latin America. Spain attempted to make good the reannexation of Santo Domingo, while France under Napoleon III launched a far more serious challenge to the Monroe Doctrine by providing the military support necessary to establish the Austrian Archduke Ferdinand Maximilian as the Emperor of Mexico. With the close of the Civil War, however, the Spanish withdrew voluntarily from Santo Domingo, and two years later, in 1867, Napoleon III, in the face of his own growing problems in Europe, and perhaps impressed by the now-available military strength of the United States, recalled his troops.

Maximilian's Empire, until its collapse, stood as the most direct threat offered thus far to the Monroe Doctrine, even though Secretary Seward in protesting the French intervention did not refer to the Doctrine by name. But the withdrawal of the French army, followed immediately by the overthrow of the unfortunate Maximilian, indicated that the United States now had the potential means to enforce the Doctrine. With the stronger national union which emerged from the ferment of the Civil War, the United States was able to take a position in the first rank of the world's powers. It is true that the American people until the close of the century concentrated most of their energies upon developing their industry and expanding their agriculture in the trans-Mississippi West, but this was a matter of choice, not weakness. Looking back, it is clear that the American nation, now united again into a more formidable Federal union, was also by 1865, rather than by 1898, already a major world power.

The years which followed the Civil War were, however, part of an era still dominated by national rather than international interests. During this age of industrial progress and western settlement, foreign affairs were on the whole neglected. In the long run, the phenomenal growth of American manufacturing and the rapid filling up of the frontier helped to turn the attention of the country outward—to new lands and markets overseas. In the generation immediately succeeding the Civil War, however, the advocates of an expansionist foreign policy received little popular support.

In view of the isolationist temper of the American people following the Civil War, it is not surprising that Secretary of State Seward met with general frustration in his attempts to add overseas possessions to the American continental domain. An ardent expansionist throughout his political career, Seward sought unavailingly during the Johnson Administration to gain Congressional support for the acquisition of naval bases or coaling stations in the Caribbean islands. Only in the Alaska treaty did his efforts meet with success, but even in that instance Congress and the country gave their approval grudgingly to what the press called "Seward's Folly" or "Seward's Icebox." In the midst of the national debate, in which the House of Representatives almost refused to vote the necessary purchase funds, Seward declared in a speech in Boston on June 24, 1867:

> Give me only this assurance, that there never be an unlawful resistance by an armed force to the President bearing the authority of the United States, and give me fifty, forty, thirty more years of life, and I will engage to give you the possession of the American continent and the control of the world.[7]

In his annual message to Congress after the purchase of Alaska had been completed, President Johnson, despite his adherence to

[7] Quoted in V. J. Farrar, *The Annexation of Russian America to the United States* (Washington, 1937), 113.

the policy of no "entangling alliances," gave a certain rhetorical backing to the imperialist versions of his expansionist-minded Secretary of State. "Comprehensive national policy," the President suggested, "would seem to sanction the acquisition and incorporation into our Federal Union of the several adjacent continental and insular communities as speedily as it can be done peacefully, lawfully, and without any violation of national justice, faith, or honor." Johnson, however, also alluded to the conviction "rapidly gaining ground in the American mind that with the increased facilities for intercommunication between all portions of the earth, the principles of free government, as embraced in our Constitution, if faithfully maintained and carried out, would prove of sufficient strength and breadth to comprehend within their sphere and influence the civilized nations of the world." [8] In the fashion of some of his most distinguished predecessors in the White House, and with an apparent indifference to certain contradictions in his own views, Johnson thus summed up the major historic themes of almost a century of American foreign policy—ideas of isolationism, mission, and manifest destiny.

Over the succeeding years, despite President Grant's own strong personal inclination to bring about the annexation of Santo Domingo, the Seward-Grant post-Civil War plans for continued American territorial growth were not realized. As an aftermath of their own recent struggle, the American people manifested a certain interest in the fate of nationalist and revolutionary movements in other parts of the world. But sympathetic observation did not lead to overt action. Thus the possibility of American intervention in the Cuban revolt was postponed another generation, and the American hope of annexing Canada was at last virtually exhausted.

In Europe, as well as in America, the era of the Civil War was a time in which movements of both a nationalistic and an imperialist nature troubled international relations. On the one hand colonial peoples and suppressed nationalities sought their freedom; on the other hand older national states were attempting to increase the extent of their territories and power. In the Old World the Poles failed in their revolt against Imperial Russia, but Germany under Bismarck became a strong national empire. On the periphery of the

8 *Messages and Papers of the Presidents*, VI, 366, 688–689.

United States domain and close to American national interests, the unhappy Cuban insurrectionists were suppressed, but the dissatisfactions of the Canadians to the north were appeased by the establishment of a stronger federation and by the grant of greater self-government within the British Empire.

By the 1870's the dominant note in international affairs was that of peace. From the Franco-Prussian War in 1870 until the Sino-Japanese War in 1894 and the Spanish-American War at the close of the century, no major conflict marred the general tranquility of the world's great powers. For the United States, President Grant in his second inaugural address to the nation expressed his "conviction that the civilized world is tending toward republicanism, or government by the people through their chosen representatives, and that our own great Republic is destined to be the guiding star of all others. . . . I believe," he added, "that our great Maker is preparing the world, in His own good time, to become one nation, speaking one language, and when armies and navies will not longer be required." [9]

Relations of the United States with both Great Britain and the Latin American countries improved, and the United States now discontinued its expansionist schemes in the Caribbean. While Great Britain remained a rival of the United States in this area as well as in the broader matter of trade with Latin America, other long-standing differences between the two countries were adjusted without resort to war. By agreeing to accept the principle of arbitration in the famous *Alabama* claims, the United States and Great Britain set a precedent for the peaceful adjudication of a major dispute between two great powers. Although England was agreeable to paying for certain damages done to American shipping by the British-built Confederate commerce raiders during the Civil War, as a part of a general restitution by the two governments of all individual citizens' claims on both sides, the British refused to accept the American contention that they should shoulder the full financial responsibility for having prolonged the Civil War. Each nation fortunately retreated from its original intransigent position and, despite the continued American propensity for "twisting the

9 *Ibid.,* VII, 221–222.

British Lion's tail" in presidential election campaigns, began to find that they had more basis for accord than enmity in their mutual relations.

In the era of peace after the Civil War, a new and stronger spirit of nationalism gradually took hold of the American people. Extending from the Atlantic to the Pacific, the country enjoyed the sense of security derived from its advantageous geographic location. Bright prospects for the future in considerable measure countered the bitterness fostered by the recent War, while the memories of that conflict in themselves helped to heighten popular sentiments of nationalism and patriotism. Even the South, looking back nostalgically upon the Lost Cause, was able to take pride in the fact that for four years it had been a nation. Continuing to cherish the Confederate flag and its associations, Southerners nevertheless were able to unite an older sectional loyalty with a new national patriotism.

In the North, stimulated by victory, the testing experience of the Civil War inspired a feeling of reverence for the nation. In place of the older legalistic, natural rights theories which had stressed the contractual nature of the Constitution and the government, American political thinkers now came to consider the nation in terms of the organic theory of Hegel and German idealist philosophy. Under these views, the state was endowed with the human qualities of personality and growth. By his loyalty and private sacrifices the citizen achieved a fuller patriotic identification with his country, while minority groups as well as individuals could be integrated within the broad homogeneous spirit of a living nationalism. Although the Indian in the West continued to be embittered, the Negro, despite the failure of Reconstruction to fulfill his hopes, remained generally loyal to the Union that had helped him to gain his freedom.

From such differing, and even discordant, elements in American life a more cohesive federal union gradually developed over the course of the post-Civil War years. This growing nationalism, in turn, became an increasingly important factor in the foreign relations of the United States. National pride and the ultrapatriotic belief that the United States had justice and right on its side in its dealings with foreign powers contributed to the aggressive tenor of

American diplomacy at the close of the century, and it also helped to smooth the way for the imperial course of the expansionists in 1898.

In the conventional sense of a foreign policy being elucidated by a series of formal exchanges or dispatches between nations, the post-Civil War and Reconstruction years have been called "the nadir of diplomacy." But in the broader sense of a foreign policy being affected by the relationships and attitudes of differing nationalities and peoples, these years were not unimportant. Despite the continued political separation from Europe, the tide of immigration to the United States increased steadily. The ten million persons who crossed the Atlantic to America in the 1880's and '90's equaled the total of all previous immigration to the United States, and by the early 1900's additional immigrants were arriving at the rate of nearly one million persons annually. In terms of numbers, the idea of America as the asylum of the oppressed of all nations had never been so real. Not only free institutions of government and religion but also the economic opportunities of factory and farm beckoned the oncoming tide. In the enthusiastic words of the *Chicago Tribune,* describing the country's future in 1864:

> Europe will open her gates like a conquered city. Her people will come forth to us subdued by admiration of our glory and envy of our perfect peace. On to the Rocky Mountains and still over to the Pacific our mighty populations will spread. . . . Our thirty millions will be tripled in thirty years.[10]

The agricultural wealth of the trans-Mississippi West and the productive power of American industry strengthened the European image of the United States as a land of opportunity. From the period of its colonial beginnings America had proved its ability to assimilate the large numbers who came to settle in the New World. Both the Christian and the democratic traditions encouraged toleration, and in no respect was American nationalism more distinctive than in its manifest willingness to absorb the varied peoples and nationalities of the Old World. At the same time many of the immigrants, in the revulsion which they felt for their European

[10] *A Century of Tribune Editorials* (Chicago, 1947), 28.

homeland, had a deep desire to help build a strong American nation. A famous cartoon of the period, captioned "Welcome to All," showed Uncle Sam ushering a motley group of immigrants to the "U.S. Ark of Refuge," outside of which there was a sign announcing: "No Oppresive Taxes; No Expensive Kings; No Compulsory Military Service; No Knouts or Dungeons." [11] In place of encouraging the expansion of the American mission abroad, the United States was winning more converts to its way of life through the policy of drawing the peoples of the Old World to the New.

Yet, as John Higham points out, the United States was never free of a dualistic attitude toward the immigrant. On the one hand he was a symbol of American Liberty attracted to the land of freedom, on the other hand he was the miserable, poverty-stricken remnant of Europe seeking physical refuge and economic security. Thus early American prejudice, mostly anti-Catholic, culminated in the nativist Know-Nothing movement of the 1850's. After the Civil War, however, confidence in the assimilative power of American nationalism returned, and in the postwar period "there was no pressing sense of the foreigner as a distinctively *national* menace. That could develop only with a loss of faith in the process of assimilation. In the postwar decades, nationalism was complacent and cosmopolitan."[12]

In this era the platforms of the two major political parties showed a continued belief in the policy of welcoming the immigrant. As late as 1892 the Republicans claimed that their party had ever been "the champion of the oppressed," which recognized the "dignity of manhood, irrespective of faith, color, or nationality." And the Democrats that year, in electing Grover Cleveland to a second term in the White House, affirmed that "This country has always been the refuge of the oppressed of every land—exiles for conscience sake." [13] But the attitude of the country toward the immigrant was already undergoing a change. Antiforeign fears had not been liquidated but were merely contained.

[11] Joseph Keppler, "Welcome to All!" *Puck,* April 28, 1880, in Allan Nevins and Frank Weitenkampf, *A Century of Political Cartoons* (New York, 1944), 126.

[12] John Higham, *Strangers in the Land* (New Brunswick, N.J., 1955), 27.

[13] *National Party Platforms, 1840–1960,* K. H. Porter and D. B. Johnson, eds. (Urbana, 1961), 94, 88.

In the 1880's the prevailing American toleration for the European masses seeking a haven in the United States began to shift. Labor, faced with the economic competition of the newcomer, was becoming antiimmigrant. Business, though it welcomed the cheap labor derived from large-scale immigration, nevertheless was fearful of the importation of radical philosophies from Europe. Hysteria over the anarchists and socialists following the Haymarket bomb episode in 1886 and the deepening economic depression of the nineties united all groups against the immigrants. Racial and religous intolerance returned along with the old fear of Catholicism and a growing dislike of the Jews and newer nationalities coming in ever-greater numbers from southern and eastern Europe. Prejudice had already manifested itself in the Chinese exclusion law of 1882, and in that year also the Federal Government for the first time in American history began to prevent the obviously unfit—the paupers, criminals, and insane—from entering the country.

Although the ethnic composition of the American population and the percentage of the foreign-born was not altered significantly in this period, the feeling grew that the new immigrants could not be assimilated into American life as easily as the peoples from northern and western Europe—English, Irish, Germans, and Scandinavians—who had made up the bulk of the immigrants before the 1880's. Strong racist and nationalist pressure developed in the country for the passage of a literacy test which would tend to discriminate particularly against poorly educated immigrants from southern and eastern European countries. Such a law was vetoed by President Cleveland in 1897, and it was not until after the First World War as the immigrant tide reached its peak that the United States passed its first comprehensive immigration restriction legislation in the nation's history.

On the whole Americans, despite the mounting prejudice of the 1880's and '90's, had moved slowly to reverse the historic traditions of welcome and asylum to the oppressed. But the close of the frontier and the slackening demand for American industrial and farm products deepened the feeling that the immigrant could no longer be easily absorbed into the mainstream of the American economy. Fear of radicalism and racial and religious prejudice also added to the belief that the newer type of immigrant could not be assimilated satisfactorily into the social and cultural life of the nation. In intellectual circles the notions of Nordic supremacy and of an Anglo-Saxon destiny became widespread, reinforcing American hostility toward all immigrants who did not trace their national origins to the countries of northern or western Europe.

By the 1890's the immigrants who had helped to build America and who had enriched and diversified American life and culture became the objects of national suspicion and fear. Despite a special popular concern over the alien radical, the bulk of the immigrants had contributed to the development of a stronger American nationalism. Forsaking the Old World with its quarrels and tribulations, the overwhelming majority of the immigrants wished to share in the richness and values of the American nation. Thus there was a paradox in the twofold way in which the immigrant affected American nationalism. By his patriotic loyalty and pride in his new homeland he played an important role in the post-Civil War recreation of a firmer federal union. Yet, at the same time, his presence also aggravated that more extreme and negative side of nationalism which is expressed in resentment and hostility toward all foreign ways or influences.

Finally, it is important to note that the changing national attitude toward the immigrant came at a time of transition in American foreign policy. The growing stress on the Anglo-Saxon character of the national mission and destiny provided notable support for the idea of a rapprochement between England and the United States in the conduct of their diplomatic affairs, and it contributed as well to an intellectual justification for imperialism. The problem of assimilating and Americanizing the immigrant at home was not, after all, unrelated to the belief that the United States should shoulder the white man's burden abroad. Moreover, it is not improbable that some of the national hysteria and concern over the immigrants, illustrated in the founding of restriction and exclusion leagues, had a counterpart in the jingoistic conduct of American foreign policy in the months preceding the Spanish-American War.

Immigration, of course, was only one of the factors underlying the revolutionary changes in American life that were coming to a head at the close of the century. The sense of security of a politically isolated, and yet economically expanding, nation was passing. An important question for the American foreign policy of the future was whether the stronger national union which had emerged from the Civil War would continue to be for the rest of the world an example of peaceful progress, or become instead the nucleus of a vast empire.

On the one hand the gaping wounds left by the Civil War had healed sufficiently for President Harrison to point to "many evidences of the increased unification of our people and of a revived national spirit. The vista that now opens to us," he declared, "is wider and more glorious than ever before. Gratification and amazement struggle for supremacy as we contemplate the population, wealth, and moral strength of our country." [14] On the other hand, as Harrison's successor Grover Cleveland, essentially a traditionalist in his views on foreign policy, was careful to stress, there were growing demands upon the United States to use its power in new and untried ways. In respect to Cuba, President Cleveland noted the pressure for American intervention and war—

a war which its advocates confidently prophesy could neither be large in its proportions nor doubtful in its issue.

The correctness of this forecast need be neither affirmed nor denied. The United States has, nevertheless, a character to maintain as a nation, which plainly dictates that right not might should be the rule of its conduct. Further, though the United States is not a nation to which peace is a necessity, it is in truth the most pacific of powers and desires nothing so much as to live in amity with all the world. Its own ample and diversified domains satisfy all possible longings for territory, preclude all dreams of conquest, and prevent any casting of covetous eyes upon neighboring regions, however attractive.[15]

Cleveland's words were a vigorous appeal to the traditions of American foreign policy. They stated an ideal, however, which was to prove difficult to maintain as the nation turned its attentions increasingly to the prospects and possibilities available to the United States overseas.

[14] *Messages and Papers of the Presidents*, IX, 211.
[15] *Ibid.*, IX, 719.

SELECTED REFERENCES

Adams, Ephraim D. *Great Britain and the American Civil War.* 2 vols. London: Longmans, Green, 1925.

Armstrong, William M. *E. L. Godkin and American Foreign Policy, 1865–1900.* New York: Bookman Associates, 1957.

Bailey, T. A. "America's Emergence as a World Power: The Myth and the Verity," *Pacific Historical Review,* XXX (February, 1961) 1–16.

Curti, Merle. *The Roots of American Loyalty.* New York: Columbia University Press, 1946.

Dulles, Foster R. *Prelude to World Power: American Diplomatic History, 1860–1900.* New York: Macmillan, 1965.

Higham, John. *Strangers in the Land: Patterns of American Nativism, 1860–1925.* New Brunswick, N.J.: Rutgers University Press, 1955.

Jordan, Donaldson, and E. J. Pratt. *Europe and the American Civil War.* Boston: Houghton Mifflin, 1931.

Kohn, Hans. *American Nationalism: An Interpretive Essay.* New York: Macmillan, 1957.

V

Expansion Abroad

American expansion by the annexation of territories overseas was a result of the Spanish-American War. With the acquisition in 1898 of Hawaii, and then the Philippines, Guam, and Puerto Rico, the United States for the first time in its history could be considered an imperial and colonial power. This new American empire, though it came as a surprise to the general citizenry, was hardly an accident of history. For at least a generation strong forces, compounded of a mixture of economics and ideology, had been pushing the American people along the way already charted by the European imperialist nations in Asia and Africa. As the country's extraordinary material development after the Civil War brought the United States to first rank among the world's powers, American business and political leaders began to think more and more in terms of extensive foreign markets and a global foreign policy.

Except in the direct sense of the acquisition of overseas possessions, American expansion abroad was, of course, neither a new policy nor a sudden interest. Historically the isolationist tradition had not precluded a search for foreign trade and markets. Indeed, an important aspect of the American struggle for independence had been the effort to gain more favorable commercial relations with Europe, while as early as the 1780's the first American merchant vessels entered the Pacific en route to China and the Far East. United States concern over outside interference with its agricultural exports had also played a part in the acquisition of Louisiana, including New Orleans, and in the resort to war in 1812. At the same time the continuing strength of the American concept of mission in the first half of the nineteenth century was evidence of a national attention to world currents of thought and political change. Thus the isolation of the United States was quickly qualified by notions of both a commercial destiny and a political mission abroad.

Although the earlier American territorial expansion of the nineteenth century had been a continental thrust into sparsely settled wilderness areas, an element of imperialism had not been lacking in the United States' relations with the Indians and Mexicans. In fact, the very term "American Empire" had been used by some of the Founding Fathers to mean an expanding American dominion over an even larger territory and population. But what Jefferson termed "an empire for liberty," or what later historians have called the agricultural imperialism of the Jeffersonians, was generally peaceful in intent. Despite the Mexican War and the aggressive American efforts to gain Cuba in the early 1850's, continental expansion and manifest destiny created a nation-state, not an imperialistic empire. Even the purchase of Alaska hardly signified a departure from the pattern of acquiring contiguous territory on the North American Continent which could some day be added to the Union as a state. After the Civil War, instead of returning to the incipient imperialist policy of the 1850's in the Caribbean, the United States concentrated its major national effort on settling the West and encouraging agriculture and manufactures. In the aftermath of the great civil and military struggle to achieve a stronger national union, a period of domestic development and consolidation seemed to be in order before the American people would be ready to look outward across the seas. Accordingly, though expansionist tendencies had not been lacking in United States experience, their full realization in the form of an imperialist empire could not come about until the War with Spain in 1898.

The roots of American expansion abroad were, in the first place, economic and ideological, rather than territorial. Although United States trade across the Pacific pointed to the desirability of naval bases and coaling stations if this growing economic stake was to be properly supported, the primary American concern was not the collection of large colonial areas. The initial small acquisitions in the Pacific—the island of Wake in 1867, the rights to the harbor of Pago Pago in Samoa in 1878, and the coaling station and naval base at Pearl Harbor in 1887—were valuable chiefly in a strategic sense. Their use was designed to improve the American economic and naval position in the Pacific.

Well before the acquisition of these first naval outposts, and a good century before Admiral Dewey's famous victory at Manila Bay, the United States had already developed tentative commercial contacts with the Far East. Sixty years after the *Empress of China* left New York harbor in 1784, the United States negotiated its initial trade treaty with China. Yankee merchants and whalers, old China hands, Protestant missionaries in Hawaii, and Commodore Matthew C. Perry's "black ships passing" were all tangible evidences of American attention to the distant reaches of the Pacific. The Perry expedition, with its economic objectives, most clearly foreshadowed the later American imperialism. Its sponsors hoped to gain trading privileges, a coaling station, and hospitality for American ships and sailors by the use of a warlike diplomacy. In the widespreading rationalizations which American political leaders invoked to justify the expedition, the economic motivation was supported by arguments derived from religion, the progress of civilization, democracy, and freedom. The opening of Japan, said Daniel Webster, was "to enable our enterprising merchants to supply the last link in that great chain which unites all nations of the world." [1]

In American opinion Japan as a backward, underdeveloped heathen nation, subject to an authoritarian form of government, was ideally suited to receive the commercial, Christianizing, and civilizing offices of the United States. In the report which he made to Congress following his voyage, Perry urged the United States to adopt a policy of imperialism. Favoring the acquisition of Pacific islands as footholds to the Far East, the Commodore also argued that the growth of American commerce now made national isolation impossible. "In the developments of the future," he declared, "the destinies of our nation must assume conspicuous attitudes; we cannot expect to be free from the ambitious longings for increased power, which are the natural concomitants of national success." In answer to the charge that an expansive policy might lead to a series of territorial aggressions and annexations, Perry replied that "after all, these events in the history and fate of nations are doubtless di-

---

[1] Quoted in W. L. Neumann, "Religion, Morality, and Freedom: The Ideological Background of the Perry Expedition," *Pacific Historical Review*, XXIII (August, 1954), 247.

rected by an overruling Providence, and probably we could not, if we would, change their course, or avert our ultimate destiny." [2]

Until the 1880's and '90's the United States was slow to follow the lead of Perry's imperialist advice. But the ambitious longings for American expansion in the Pacific never died out completely and were easily susceptible of renewal. In the same way American interest in Latin America, though it did not approach again the expansionist ferment of the 1850's until the coming of the War with Spain, was quiescent and waiting. United States anxiety over the Caribbean area continued after the Civil War but, in the words of one scholar, "for thirty years it was more like an underground river than a surface stream." [3] Although Secretary Seward's and President Grant's plans for Caribbean colonies or protectorates were rebuffed, in the 1880's James G. Blaine was able to launch his idea of a Pan American Conference. Through closer trade and cultural relations with the Latin American nations, Blaine hoped to secure better markets for American exports, thereby lessening the unfavorable balance of trade between the United States and the neighboring republics to the South. Gradually Pan Americanism became coupled with the Monroe Doctrine as an expression of paternalistic United States policies toward Latin America in the early years of the twentieth century.

In the eighties and nineties a succession of diplomatic incidents involving Latin American nations, followed by the Cleveland Administration's aggressive stand against Great Britain in its boundary dispute with Venezuela in 1895, testified to the United States' intentions of maintaining its hegemony in the New World. Cleveland's Secretary of State Richard Olney did not favor a policy of American colonization, but he believed that the time had come for the United States to exercise a commanding role in world affairs. The growing need of American industry for more and greater markets, Olney concluded, might be satisfied most naturally by increas-

[2] *Narrative of the Expedition of an American Squadron to the China Seas and Japan*, F. L. Hawks, ed. (Washington, 1856), II, 177–178.

[3] R. W. Van Alstyne, *The Rising American Empire* (New York, 1960), 161.

ing United States exports to Latin America. By his bold claim
restating the Monroe Doctrine—"To-day the United States is practically sovereign on this continent, and its fiat is law upon the subjects to which it confines its interposition"—Olney made it clear
to Great Britain and the world that in the instance of the Venezuela
boundary the question was one in which the United States' "honor
and its interests are involved and the continuance of which it can
not regard with indifference." [4] In essence, as Walter LaFeber
points out, Olney was using the Monroe Doctrine "as the catchall
slogan which justified protecting what the United States considered
as its own interests. If the Monroe Doctrine had not existed, Olney's
note would have been written anyway, only the term American
Self-Interest would have been used instead of the Monroe Doctrine." [5]

Olney's unfriendly note, followed by Cleveland's warlike message to Congress challenging Great Britain's unwillingness to arbi-
trate the boundary dispute, expressed the rising jingoistic mood of
the country. A few months later this climate of opinion was to cul-
minate in the demand to free Cuba and annex the Philippines. Yet,
with all its implications for the end of isolation and the turn to
imperialism, Cleveland's bellicosity toward Britain was essentially
negative and political. It gained no economic benefits abroad, and
it did little to allay farmer-labor discontent at home. In contrast to the Cleveland bluster, the imperialism favored by the preceding Harrison Administration seemed in retrospect to have
promised greater material rewards. An aggressive American expansion in new areas overseas might offer more tangible returns than
a policy of protecting traditional American interests within the
sphere of the Monroe Doctrine.

The economic background underlying American expansionist
ideology not only was fundamental, but it has also become widely
familiar. Historians as well as some contemporary observers have

[4] *Papers Relating to the Foreign Relations of the United States, 1895* (Washington, 1896), I, 558, 552.
[5] Walter La Feber, *The New Empire* (Ithaca, N.Y., 1963), 260.

discerned a more than incidental connection in the passing of the frontier, the continuing hard times of the nineties, the surge of industrialism, and the turn to imperialism and navalism. Certainly there was little doubt that American economic development overseas was on the threshold of a new age of expansion. Though American exports had been growing since at least the 1840's, the balance of foreign trade was generally unfavorable to the United States until after the Civil War and Reconstruction. Despite the fact that the United States remained a net debtor nation in the nineteenth century, however, it still was able to furnish probably 90 percent of its own capital besides being able to make modest investments abroad. In the 1880's the United States led the world in wheat production, and in the next decade it led, or nearly led, in the production of coal, iron, and steel. Historically the most important American exports were cotton, wheat, and tobacco, but as the balance of trade shifted in America's favor, the percentage of manufactured goods in its exports steadily increased. In 1897 the value of manufactured articles exported exceeded that of those imported for the first time. That same year the margin by which the value of exports exceeded imports was the greatest in history, and a year later, in 1898, the margin had doubled. The ever-increasing American population, which rose more than 100 percent in the generation between the Civil War and the War with Spain, was able to consume nine-tenths of American products, but the other tenth was far from unimportant and amounted to perhaps a billion dollars by 1897.

Despite the overall gains of the American economy and the impressive rise in American exports, especially in the category of factory products, the three decades of the 1870's, '80's, and '90's were plagued by generally falling prices, recurring financial panics, and periods of economic depression. The American frontier seemed at best an imperfect safety valve for the economic problems of farmers and workingmen. Farmer-labor discontent, caused in large part by the declining prices and wages of the period, was reflected in the political radicalism of the Populist and Socialist parties. At the same time each succeeding panic and depression seemed to intensify the search of American business for new markets. In urging an expansionist policy upon the United States, businessmen did not insist on territorial acquisitions but, if the course of European imperialism was an example, colonies were likely to be associated with trade.

By the closing decades of the nineteenth century economic penetration into the less developed, outlying areas of the world was not an unattractive possibility for the United States. To probably the larger share of the American public, expansion abroad, if it was necessary to preserve private enterprise and free competition at home, was preferable to European concepts of socialism or drastic government regulation. The economic stewardship implied in the business philosophy of Andrew Carnegie's "Gospel of Wealth," when carried overseas, became a part of the white man's burden. In the same way political philosophies of benevolent aid or paternalistic regulation of business were easily projected to cover an official expansionist policy of securing new outlets and markets for American domestic surpluses. Tariff reciprocity to widen markets for American exports was as logical a policy as high duties to protect infant American industries.

Though an expansionist program seemed to offer a plausible solution to some of the economic ills of the 1880's and '90's, the business and producing classes were not the most ardent spokesmen for American imperialism. Instead, its first and most articulate support was found among an interesting elite of publicists and politicians, missionaries and navalists, professors and moral philosophers. The expansionist ideology which met with the favor of these influential individuals was a mixture of the philosophies of manifest destiny, Darwinian evolution, Anglo-Saxon racism, economic determinism, militarism and navalism, nationalism and patriotism. Many of those who favored an imperial course for the United States merely justified and rationalized the succession of events that took place after 1898. But among the expansionists were a small number of important precursors who argued for such a national policy while it was still in the process of becoming a reality.

The serious and systematic formulation of an American doctrine of imperialism began in the 1880's. Midway in that decade John Fiske, a popular interpreter of Darwinian evolution and American historical subjects, published in *Harper's Magazine* his well-known lecture which used as its title the old slogan "Manifest Destiny." The new manifest destiny of the United States, Fiske believed, was world leadership. It was the role of the Anglo-Saxon nations to exercise political domination, and this historic tradition plus the recent industrial progress of the United States required the country to develop a colonial policy. In Fiske's eyes the coming imperialism was to be peaceful and benevolent, a result of American industrial power and Anglo-Saxon leadership, instead of war.

The Anglo-Saxon mystique which Fiske helped to popularize derived much of its strength from Darwinian notions of a competition of peoples and races. Darwin himself, in his *Descent of Man*, seemed to accept the view that "the wonderful progress of the United States, as well as the character of the people, are the results of natural selection; the more energetic, restless, and courageous men from all parts of Europe having emigrated during the last ten or twelve generations to that great country, and having there succeeded best." [6] After the 1880's an Anglo-Saxon interpretation of American history and democracy reigned supreme, at least in intellectual circles. Overcoming the politicians' traditional "twisting of the Lion's tail" in order to cater to anti-British feeling among the Irish-American voters, this Anglo-Saxonism gradually contributed to a new Anglo-American rapprochement in diplomatic circles. Thus, rather than compete for markets and colonies, Great Britain and the United States were willing to work out an amicable division of their respective spheres of influence as a means of containing the expansion of the German Empire.

Fiske's own lecture on manifest destiny was delivered more than twenty times in the United States before it was published in a book as well as an article in 1885, but still "Fiske as a spokesman of expansion was but a small voice compared with the Reverend Josiah Strong." [7] A tireless writer and speaker and a born missionary, Strong published his slender volume entitled *Our Country: Its Possible Future and Its Present Crisis* (1885), under the auspices of the American Home Missionary Society, primarily to solicit funds for their cause. On the title page of his book Strong quoted Emerson's words: "We live in a new and exceptional age. America is

[6] Charles Darwin, *The Descent of Man* (New York, 1888), 142.
[7] Richard Hofstadter, *Social Darwinism in American Thought, 1860–1915* (Philadelphia, 1944), 153.

another name for opportunity. Our whole history appears like a last effort of the Divine Providence in behalf of the human race." To participate in this final struggle, the United States enjoyed the unrivaled material resources of the West as well as the probability of containing within its borders "the larger portion of the Anglo-Saxon race for generations to come." At the same time, however, there were dangers to American future progress stemming from immigration, Catholicism, Mormonism, intemperance, socialism, urbanism, excessive wealth, and materialism. The home missionary movement's function was to correct or alleviate these ills so that the nation could face its most pressing future problem. With the exhaustion of the unoccupied lands around the globe and especially in the American West, where they had been the basis of United States prosperity, the world was entering upon "the final competition of races, for which the Anglo-Saxon is being schooled." Strong was confident that the Anglo-Saxon race, the divine depository of the eternal principles of Christianity and civil liberty, was destined to spread over the earth. As the principal home of this race, the seat of its coming power and influence, it was the duty of the United States to assume the leadership and responsibility for the future progress of the world.[8]

The concept of an imperial mission or destiny for the United States, as set forth in Fiske's and Strong's Anglo-Saxon interpretations of history, was part of an international or world outlook expressed by a small but growing number of American scholars and intellectuals. In the closing years of the nineteenth century Frederick Jackson Turner's frontier hypothesis, Brooks Adams' cyclical interpretation, and Alfred Thayer Mahan's stress on the role of seapower in history could all be regarded as important efforts to look at the American experience within the wider framework of world history and geography. Pervading the ideas of these oddly assorted and varied men was a common feeling of impending, and even cataclysmic, changes which would drastically alter the future course of the United States. As students of the past Turner, Adams, and Mahan all seemed to share the view that the period in which they lived and worked was a dividing point or a watershed in American historical development.

Turner, a young professor of history at the University of Wis-

8 Josiah Strong, *Our Country* (New York, 1885), 168, 175.

consin in the 1890's, is more commonly associated with the concept of isolationism than of imperialism in United States history. The nostalgia for the older frontier ways of rural America implied in his celebrated frontier hypothesis has been criticized for inculcating a nationalistic, provincial attitude among scholars and even the general public. But Turner, in his epochal paper, "The Significance of the Frontier in American History," made the point that by the 1890's the United States was no longer unique. The course of history had finally caught up with the American people. In the past, free, or nearly free, land to the west had offered America the opportunity for economic expansion, and this economic freedom in turn had been the major influence in the development of American political and social institutions—democracy, equality, individualism, nationalism. "And now," he declared, "four centuries from the discovery of America, at the end of a hundred years of life under the Constitution, the frontier has gone, and with its going has closed the first period of American history." [9] In another paper, written somewhat earlier, Turner had noted the traditional American isolation from Europe. "But it is one of the profoundest lessons that history has to teach," he pointed out, "that political relations, in a highly developed civilization, are inextricably connected with economic relations. Already there are signs of a relaxation of our policy of commercial isolation. Reciprocity is a word that meets with increasing favor from all parties. But once fully afloat on the sea of worldwide economic interests, we shall soon develop political interests." [10]

The connection of this demise of American isolation, along with the passing of the frontier, to the onset of American expansion abroad Turner clarified in an article he wrote during the bitterly contested Bryan-McKinley presidential campaign of 1896. Under the title "The Problem of the West," Turner made explicit this relationship between the older American westward expansion and the coming American imperialism:

For nearly three hundred years the dominant fact in American life has been expansion. With the settlement of the Pacific coast and the occupa-

[9] *Frontier and Section: Selected Essays of Frederick Jackson Turner*, R. A. Billington, ed. (Englewood Cliffs, N.J., 1961), 62.
[10] *Ibid.*, 23.

tion of the free lands, this movement has come to a check. That these energies of expansion will no longer operate would be a rash prediction; and the demands for a vigorous foreign policy, for an inter-oceanic canal, for a revival of our power upon the seas, and for the extension of American influence to outlying islands and adjoining countries, are indications that the movement will continue. The stronghold of these demands lies west of the Alleghanies.[11]

Although Turner's ideas were a part of the climate of opinion affecting the formulation of American foreign policy, it is difficult to measure the influence of this academic scholar on the expansionists of the 1890's. Yet he undoubtedly impressed his views on both Theodore Roosevelt and Woodrow Wilson. One of the merits of Turner's essays was, as Roosevelt said, that he "put into definite shape a good deal of thought which has been floating around rather loosely."[12] Wilson, a close friend of Turner's who brought the frontier hypothesis to a wider audience in his own popular writings, admitted readily that "All I ever wrote on the subject came from him."[13] Certainly it seems true that, in his awareness of the relationship between the changing ideas of American foreign policy and past American experience, no scholar was more perceptive than Turner. And although his writings did not rival those of Fiske or Strong in reaching a popular audience, his ideas much more than theirs helped provide a key to an historical understanding of American foreign policy in the twentieth century.

While Turner was content to suggest his frontier hypothesis as an explanation of United States history, Brooks Adams, the lineal descendant of two American Presidents, offered his "law" as an interpretation of all past history. *The Law of Civilization and Decay*, which he published in 1895, analyzed history in economic terms, or more specifically in terms of the influence of the major trade routes of the world such as the Mediterranean Sea. Nations rose and fell, Adams contended, in the rhythm of their commercial growth and decay. In the cyclical movement from barbarism to civilization, materialistic and economic values became predominant,

11 *Ibid.*, 74.
12 *The Letters of Theodore Roosevelt*, E. E. Morison, ed. (Cambridge, Mass., 1951–1954), I, 363.
13 Quoted in La Feber, *The New Empire*, 71.

while the martial and imaginative arts declined, and the amount of surplus energy in society was dissipated.

In proportion as movement accelerates societies consolidate, and as societies consolidate they pass through a profound intellectual change. Energy ceases to find vent through the imagination, and takes the form of capital; hence as civilizations advance the imaginative temperament tends to disappear, while the economic instinct is fostered, and thus substantially new varieties of men come to possess the world.[14]

Alarmed by the Panic of 1893, Adams was convinced that the class of American bankers and capitalists, whom he regarded as notably selfish and unfit, was pushing the United States toward the realization of his law. Only some drastic political and economic shift could stave off an impending collapse, and here Adams became an advocate of the expansionist policies that were adopted after 1898, and which he spelled out in greater detail in his own later books, *America's Economic Supremacy* and *The New Empire*. In brief, Adams believed that the United States should assume the old commercial role of England and the European centers of trade, develop its governmental and administrative efficiency and leadership, and be prepared for war.

Brooks Adams' espousal of the martial virtues as a means to the renewal of American energies found its strongest political support in the ideas and activities of his friend Theodore Roosevelt. But Roosevelt was primarily a man of action, elevated to the Presidency by the accident of McKinley's assassination. The militaristic logic and strategy which he encouraged, and which was essential to the coming American imperialism, had as its most noted philosopher, therefore, not T. R. but the celebrated naval officer and historian Alfred Thayer Mahan.

Among his fellow expansionists of the 1890's Mahan was probably the most influential. Through his books and many magazine articles, and through his intimate association with American statesmen and politicians, he was able to affect public policy. An

[14] Brooks Adams, *The Law of Civilization and Decay* (New York, 1895), 245.

able popularizer and propagandist of the navalism that was already spreading in Europe and the United States, Mahan's writings, in turn, further encouraged the advocates of a big navy and imperialism in Germany, England, and Japan, as well as in the United States. More than the other American expansionists of the period, Mahan accepted the Prussian deification of war and looked askance upon a foreign policy that was not backed up by the threat of force. War, which he thought of as a moral system, was simply a nation's willingness to stand by its principles to the bitter end.

Early in his career Mahan had been critical of James G. Blaine's aggressive diplomacy, and he had also originally advocated a larger navy mainly as a means of keeping American ports open to neutral foreign trade in time of war. But the point of view increasingly popular in naval circles that a powerful American fleet was needed to protect American exports and markets abroad, was consistently championed by Mahan from the late 1880's until his death in 1914. Mahan, along with Benjamin F. Tracy, Secretary of the Navy under Benjamin Harrison, has often been cited as an intellectual godfather of the modern American navy. A decade before the building program of the 1880's and the administrative reforms carried out by Secretary Tracy, however, the *Annual Report* of an earlier Secretary of the Navy was already pointing out that "Without foreign commerce we must sink into inferiority; and without a Navy amply sufficient for this purpose, all the profits of our surplus productions will be transferred from the coffers of our own to those of foreign capitalists." [15]

Mahan himself, despite his pleading for a big navy, did not think of navalism as an end in itself but as a necessary adjunct of the expanding American commercial and industrial order. In 1890, as a Captain assigned to duty at the Naval War College in Newport, Rhode Island, he published his first book, *The Influence of Sea Power upon History, 1660–1783*. This work, of which Theodore Roosevelt wrote: "I am greatly in error if it does not become a classic," [16] developed with a wealth of historical detail drawn largely from English history the thesis that naval strength was the all-important factor in the rise or fall of a great nation. At this

---

15 *Report of the Secretary of the Navy* (Washington, 1877), 8–9.
16 Quoted in G. T. Davis, *A Navy Second to None* (New York, 1940), 73–74.

time, Mahan, who now became a publicist and historian as well as a naval officer, also wrote the first of his many popular articles advocating an imperialist policy for the United States. Under the title "The United States Looking Outward," Mahan contended that Americans must henceforth venture beyond the confines of their own secure and protected home market. For American industries, he wrote, "outside, beyond the broad seas, there are the markets of the world, that can be entered and controlled only by a vigorous contest. . . ." And, he concluded, "it is safe to predict that, when the opportunities for gain abroad are understood, the course of American enterprise will cleave a channel by which to reach them."[17]

Central to Mahan's strategic ideas regarding American foreign policy was an interoceanic canal across the Isthmus of Panama. Such a canal, however, unless it were protected by adequate naval power and bases in the Caribbean and at the Hawaiian Islands, would only be a source of weakness to the United States and a focal point of attack in time of war. With the Isthmus pierced, however, Mahan was confident that the ensuing world trade which would be drawn to American waters would cause the isolation and indifference of the United States to foreign nations to pass away.

Whether they will or no, Americans must now begin to look outward. The growing production of the country demands it. An increasing volume of public sentiment demands it. The position of the United States, between the two Old Worlds and the two great oceans, makes the same claim, which will soon be strengthened by the creation of the new link joining the Atlantic and the Pacific. The tendency will be maintained and increased by the growth of the European colonies in the Pacific, by the advancing civilization of Japan, and by the rapid peopling of our Pacific States with men who have all the aggressive spirit of the advanced line of national progress. Nowhere does a vigorous foreign policy find more favor than among the people west of the Rocky Mountains.[18]

In the rhetoric of the advocates of the so-called "large policy" of expansionism in United States diplomacy, imperialism and navalism were used interchangeably as cause and effect. Thus it was argued that a great navy was needed to defend overseas ex-

[17] A. T. Mahan, *The Interest of America in Sea Power* (Boston, 1911), 4–5.
[18] *Ibid.*, 21–22.

pansion, and the resultant imperialism, in turn, was used to justify still larger naval appropriations. On the one hand an interoceanic canal, naval bases, and coaling stations were necessary for the efficiency of the navy; on the other hand the navy was needed to protect outlying possessions. Beneath this seeming paradox, and lessening somewhat the contradictory nature of the reasoning of Mahan and his fellow navalists, was their contention that imperialism and navalism both were justified in the last analysis by America's economic needs as an industrially expanding nation in search of foreign markets. Accordingly Mahan, though he shared the other expansionists' enthusiasm for the concept of an Anglo-Saxon world destiny, was more realistic and practical in relating American expansion to the national economic interest. Aware that the expansionists' pleas of an American world mission were being criticized for seeming suspiciously like a cloak for national self-interest, Mahan frankly faced the dilemma. "Let us not shrink," he wrote in 1893, "from pitting a broad self-interest against the narrow self-interest to which some would restrict us." [19]

From the retrospect of the twentieth century it is easy to see why the views of Mahan and his fellow expansionists of the 1890's proved so congenial to the American political leaders who carried out the imperial and colonial policies which followed United States success in the Spanish-American War. Congressmen in their debates on foreign and naval affairs consistently plagiarized not only Mahan's ideas, but also his words and phrases, and their speeches resounded to the refrains of manifest destiny and the Anglo-Saxon mission. Both Mahan and Brooks Adams, the prime advocates of imperialism, were also the intimate associates or close friends of a small Washington society of wealthy and cultured scholars in politics of whom John Hay, Theodore Roosevelt, and Henry Cabot Lodge were the most important. As a member of the House Naval Affairs Committee, Lodge gave unfailing support to larger appropriations for the navy, which he regarded as both an advance agent and defender of American foreign commerce. In reply to critics of this policy Lodge declared that "for the protection of American business interests, and American citizens in all parts

[19] *Ibid.*, 51.

of the world wherever they may go, we want to have the American flag on American men-of-war." [20] As Assistant Secretary of the Navy in the McKinley Administration, Roosevelt was in a strategic spot to exercise pressure in behalf of the naval policies of his friends Lodge and Mahan, while John Hay as Ambassador to England and then as Secretary of State was, of course, in the most influential governmental position of all among his circle of expansionist friends.

Hay, Lodge, and Roosevelt, "the three musketeers of war," formed the nucleus of a Washington elite of younger politicians and professional diplomats who made up what has been called appropriately "Roosevelt's salon." [21] United by a generally conservative political outlook, but restless intellectually, the members of the group were disturbed by President McKinley's complacency in the face of the popular discontents of the 1890's. With no great projects to occupy their minds or energies, they turned with relief and enthusiasm to expansion abroad and to what Hay himself termed the "splendid little war" with Spain. Though staunch nationalists, Roosevelt and his friends were far from isolationists. Convinced that their country could never act wrongly or unjustly in international affairs, they were ready to accept the challenge of war, especially when they believed that important questions of national pride and interest were at stake.

To the American people in general, the War with Spain was an idealistic crusade for the liberation of Cuba in which even the radical and antimilitaristic Populists enlisted enthusiastically. But to Roosevelt and his fellow expansionists of 1898, though they were not unmindful of the humanitarian considerations at stake, the war had a deeper strategic meaning. When the increasing United States pressure upon Spain finally resulted in hostilities, the American Pacific fleet, in accord with Mahan's precepts and Roosevelt's and McKinley's orders, was ready for its famous dash from Hong Kong to Manila Bay. At home Albert J. Beveridge, soon to be elected United States Senator from Indiana, gave an accurate forecast of the new American foreign policy in his letters and speeches: "The Philippines are logically our first target. . . . There

20 April 16, 1892, *Congressional Record*, 52 Cong., 1 Sess., 3362.
21 Matthew Josephson, *The President Makers* (New York, 1940), 21–28, 142–144.

is no such thing as isolationism in the world today. They say that Cuba is not contiguous; . . . that the Philippines are not contiguous. They are contiguous. Our navy will make them contiguous." In Beveridge's mind there was no question of the inevitability of what was taking place in the Pacific. "It is God's great purpose," he said, "made manifest in the instincts of our race, whose present phase is our personal profit, but whose far-off end is the redemption of the world and the Christianization of mankind." Striking a more prosaic note and becoming more specific, Beveridge also declared:

American factories are making more than the American people can use; American soil is producing more than they can consume. Fate has written our policy for us; the trade of the world must and shall be ours. . . . Our institutions will follow our flag on the wings of our commerce. And American law, American order, American civilization, and the American flag will plant themselves on shores hitherto bloody and benighted, but by those agencies of God henceforth to be made beautiful and bright.[22]

To Beveridge and his co-imperialists the policies which they advocated, and which they did so much to put into effect, were simply the result of a revived manifest destiny—of forces beyond the nation's control. But this interpretation, however much it was urged by Roosevelt, Hay, Mahan, and some of the nation's press, was open to considerable question. While it was true that the economic development of the United States had brought the country into increasing contact with world affairs, it was by no means so certain that such contact had to result in territorial acquisitions overseas. This latter policy, so pregnant with meaning for the future of American foreign affairs, might not have been carried out at all had it not been for the skillful propaganda of the expansionists with their repeated emphasis on the inevitable workings of manifest destiny.

In angry rejoinder to such reasoning William Jennings Bryan, the Democratic standard bearer, complained that "Destiny is not a matter of chance; it is a matter of choice. . . ." It "is the subterfuge

22 Quoted in C. G. Bowers, *Beveridge and the Progressive Era* (Boston, 1932), 69–70, 76.

of the invertebrate, who, lacking the courage to oppose error, seeks some plausible excuse for supporting it." [23] Bryan expressed views characteristic of many of the Populists and Democrats and of idealists and reformers generally. These segments of the public had been willing to back the Spanish-American War as a humanitarian crusade, but they drew away from supporting the ensuing imperialism. Then, with the sudden ending of the War by the close of the summer, their attention shifted from Cuba to the question of the Philippines. In the debate over whether the United States should annex the islands, a good deal of the moral force and fervor with which American public opinion had aided the Cuban cause was transferred to the rising anti-imperialist movement. Although the anti-imperialists were not able to defeat the peace treaty with its provisions for the acquisition of Puerto Rico, Guam, and all the Philippines, they were able to bring the issue of imperialism into the open and to raise some national doubt as to whether it was in accord with the historic traditions of the Republic. For the first time in their history the American people were called upon to decide the novel question of whether the Constitution followed the flag across the Pacific, and of whether democracy could be preserved at home in its new imperial setting.

The anti-imperialist movement, though never well organized outside of Boston and a few other large cities, included some of the most distinguished statesmen and men of letters in America. William Dean Howells, Mark Twain, William Vaughn Moody, and Thomas Bailey Aldrich all opposed colonial expansion, while Samuel Bowles, E. L. Godkin, and Finley Peter Dunne were important journalistic critics. In the Democratic party Bryan and eight members of Cleveland's Cabinet, including the former President and his Secretary of State Richard Olney, were ranged against imperialism. Among Republicans it was mostly the liberal reform element of elder statesmen carrying on the old antislavery traditions who protested McKinley's annexationist policies. Typical of this group was Carl Schurz, who had long been an opponent of the type of aggressive militarism and navalism that he now publicly linked to Theodore Roosevelt. In the press and on the platform Schurz repeatedly attacked the new imperial policy as contrary to the funda-

[23] *Speeches of William Jennings Bryan* (New York, 1909), II, 11, 47.

mental principles and ideals of American democratic government. Imperialism was contrary to the true mission of the American people. The United States could not assume a universal responsibility for every place and people in the world, or American democracy itself would break down. "No, do not deceive yourselves," he pleaded.

If we turn that war which was so solemnly commended to the favor of mankind as a generous war of liberation and humanity into a victory for conquest and self-aggrandizement, we shall have thoroughly forfeited our moral credit with the world. Professions of unselfish virtue and benevolence, proclamations of noble humanitarian purposes coming from us will never, never be trusted again.[24]

In the moral fervor of his onslaught upon the new imperial policy, Schurz was joined by such academic figures as David Starr Jordan, President of Stanford University, and William Graham Sumner, the Yale professor and author of *The Conquest of the United States by Spain*. Sumner and Jordan believed that an aggressive foreign policy, leading to militarism and war, would be the death of American institutions. The imperialists, Sumner noted, now were engaged in repudiating the very American traditions he had been accused of flouting, and he predicted that through imperialism the United States would eventually lose its freedom and democracy. "The answer is: war, debt, taxation, diplomacy, a grand governmental system, pomp, glory, a big army and navy, lavish expenditures, political jobbery—in a word, imperialism." [25]

While there was little explicit opposition to imperialism on the part of businessmen or labor leaders, Andrew Carnegie was a staunch critic and Samuel Gompers showed some interest. On the whole, however, the anti-imperialist movement was based more on abstract political and ideological principles than on economic, religious, constitutional, or humanitarian considerations. Imperialism was opposed as contrary to the traditions of American democratic government and the foreign policies of more than a century.

[24] *Speeches, Correspondence and Political Papers of Carl Schurz*, Frederic Bancroft, ed. (New York, 1913), VI, 26.

[25] W. G. Sumner, *The Conquest of the United States by Spain* (Boston, 1899), 25.

The abandonment of these principles in favor of imitating the ways of the Old World, the anti-imperialists believed, would destroy the Republic.

Although the anti-imperialists made their strongest appeal to American traditions, imperialists also called upon these traditions in order to bolster their view of American foreign policy. Democracy, the imperialists maintained, could be extended only to a people fitted to receive it. Self-government depended on a nation's capacity for political action, and if a people were not ready for independence, they must undergo a period of political tutelage and protection. Thus the imperialists joined the American conception of manifest destiny with Rudyard Kipling's call to the Anglo-Saxon nations to take up the white man's burden. In the curious reasoning of an official United States commission to the Philippines, "American sovereignty was only another name for the liberty of the Filipinos." [26]

From the state of Kansas in the Midwest the youthful journalist William Allen White, in an editorial in his *Emporia Gazette* on the first anniversary of the sinking of the *Maine*, wrote:

> It was probably intended in the beginning that the Anglo-Saxon should conquer the Latin. The conquest has been going on for four centuries. The completion of the manifest destiny of the race could not be postponed long. And yet thousands of people cannot help longing for the old order. They cannot but feel that something good is gone and that this deepening of responsibilities brings a hardship with it and a loss of the old-time individual freedom. For every American is not only his own master now—as he was a year ago—but he is master, as much as a man can ever be another's master, of twenty million people of lower races and inferior intelligence. And the master has lost the freedom that the slave has found.

A month later, in commenting on the news of riots in Havana, White expressed the opinion that the United States would have to keep on policing the island. The Cubans were not, and could not

[26] Schurman Commission, quoted in A. K. Weinberg, *Manifest Destiny* (Baltimore, 1935), 295.

be, really free. Only Anglo-Saxon nations could actually govern themselves, he maintained.

It is the Anglo-Saxon's manifest destiny to go forth as a world conqueror. He will take possession of all the islands of the sea. He will exterminate the peoples he cannot subjugate. This is what fate holds for the chosen people. It is so written. Those who would protest will find their objections overruled. It is to be.[27]

A spate of imperialist books published in the early 1900's helped to acquaint the American people with their recently acquired world responsibilities. The Reverend Josiah Strong in his new work *Expansion* rejoiced that the ideas he had expressed earlier in *Our Country* had come true. At Columbia University Franklin H. Giddings, professor of sociology, took issue with Sumner's thesis that democracy and imperialism were incompatible. The future progress of world civilization, Giddings wrote in his *Democracy and Empire,* would be determined by the extension of American ideals of liberty and equality. Drawing upon the theory of biological evolution, Giddings decided that political progress depended on the absorption of smaller states and colonies into large democratic empires.

In 1900 Brooks Adams, under the bold title *America's Economic Supremacy,* published his analysis of the new imperialism. The Adams version united economic arguments with the strategy of power politics advocated by Roosevelt and Mahan. England and the United States, he believed, were now more than ever essential to each other, while an increasing American entanglement abroad was inevitable. Although the Anglo-Saxon had been the most individual of races, as territorial expansion ceased and economic competition quickened, men consolidated into denser masses and individualism declined. American prosperity hitherto had been due to "the liberal margin of profit" resulting from the extension of the frontier, but now the time had come when the surplus must be sold abroad. "Today," Adams wrote, "the nation has to elect whether to continue to expand, cost what it may, or to resign itself to the approach of a relatively stationary period, when competition will force it to abandon the individual for the collective mode of life." [28] In a later

[27] *Emporia Gazette,* February 16, March 20, 1899, in *The Editor and His People: Editorials by William Allen White,* H. O. Mahin, ed. (New York, 1924), 304–306.

[28] Brooks Adams, *America's Economic Supremacy* (New York, 1900), 48–49.

volume, *The New Empire,* Adams continued to spell out his prescrip-
tion for American imperialism. The seat of energy and empire, he
wrote, was already being transferred from Europe to America, but he
noted:

> If the New Empire should develop, it must be an enormous complex
> mass, to be administered only by means of a cheap, elastic, and simple
> machinery; an old and clumsy mechanism must, sooner or later, collapse,
> and in sinking may involve a civilization. If these deductions are sound,
> there is but one great boon which the passing generation can confer upon
> its successors: it can aid them to ameliorate that servitude to tradition
> which has so often retarded submission to the inevitable until too late.[29]

The younger Adams, it may be said, was more sanguine of imperialism than his older brother Henry who, as early as February,
1901, was writting to Brooks in disillusionment over the possibility
of the United States assuming the leadership of the world. "This
country cannot possibly run it," he declared.

> I incline now to anti-imperialism, and very strongly to anti-militarism.
> I incline to let the machine smash, and see what pieces are worth saving
> afterwards. I incline to let England sink; to let Germany and Russia try to
> run the machine, and to stand on our own internal resources alone.[30]

Voicing a similar sense of alarm over the international situation,
Henry Cabot Lodge confided to Theodore Roosevelt:

> If we have a strong and well equipped navy, I do not believe Germany
> will attack us. At the same time there is a fundamental danger which
> arises from our rapid growth economically. We are putting a terrible
> pressure on Europe, and the situation may produce war at any time. The
> economic forces will not be the ostensible cause of trouble, but they will
> be the real cause, and no one can tell where the break will come.[31]

Unlike his brother Henry, Brooks Adams discerned the significant role that their friend Theodore Roosevelt was destined to
fill as President, and the even greater importance and connection
with American foreign policy of the Roosevelt version of Progressivism. Much of the imperialist argument as it had been developed

[29] Brooks Adams, *The New Empire* (New York, 1902), 211.

[30] February 7, 1901, in H. D. Cater, *Henry Adams and His Friends* (Boston,
1947), 504.

[31] March 30, 1901, in *Selections from the Correspondence of Theodore
Roosevelt and Henry Cabot Lodge* (New York, 1925), I, 487.

since the 1890's fitted in well with the Progressives' own philosophy of government. A number of historians have noted the linkage of the two movements. According to Robert Osgood, "The spirit of imperialism was an exaltation of duty above rights, of collective welfare above individual self-interest, the heroic values as opposed to materialism, action instead of logic, the natural impulse rather than the pallid intellect." [32] In his book *Democracy and Reaction,* the English critic L. T. Hobhouse maintained that by the close of the nineteenth century "a positive theory of the State in domestic affairs was matched by a positive theory of Empire, and the way was made straight for Imperialism. . . ." [33] "Most important," as William E. Leuchtenburg has pointed out, "imperialism and progressivism flourished together because they were both expressions of the same philosophy of government, a tendency to judge any action not by the means employed but by the results achieved, a worship of definitive action for action's sake . . . and an almost religious faith in the democratic mission of America." [34]

While imperialism in the more active sense of the acquisition of overseas dependencies waned, there was no slackening of American economic and political interests abroad. Dollar diplomacy in the Caribbean area, military intervention in Latin America, and Theodore Roosevelt's own attempts at global peacemaking at Portsmouth and Algeciras were examples of continued American involvement overseas. Roosevelt himself added his so-called corollary to the Monroe Doctrine to the classic list of Presidential pronouncements on American foreign policy. By Roosevelt's injunction the United States asserted the right to interfere in the internal affairs of the Latin American republics if this became necessary to prevent outside intervention by a European power. In practice the United States proposed to act as a collector when financial or political disorders in Latin America endangered its debts to European creditor nations. In the Western Hemisphere, Roosevelt declared, "the adherence of the United States to the Monroe Doctrine may force the United States, however reluctantly, in flagrant cases of such wrong-

[32] R. E. Osgood, *Ideals and Self-Interest in America's Foreign Relations* (Chicago, 1953), 47.

[33] L. T. Hobhouse, *Democracy and Reaction* (New York, 1905), 12.

[34] W. E. Leuchtenburg, "Progressivism and Imperialism," *Mississippi Valley Historical Review,* XXXIX (December, 1952), 500.

doing or impotence, to the exercise of an international police power." [35] According to the Roosevelt version of the Monroe Doctrine, the corollary of nonintervention in the Americas by European states was to be the direct intervention of the United States. Thus in the Caribbean as well as in the Pacific, the Spanish-American War encouraged an aggressive American economic and military policy to go along with territorial expansion.

Looking back on these early years of the new century, the political scientist Charles E. Merriam summed up the change that had taken place in the ideology of American foreign policy:

> The acquisition of overseas dependencies floated the nation gently into the swift current which was certain to lead to the mingling of international waters. Doctrines of international duty and mission were developed and widely, although not universally accepted. America slowly awakened to international consciousness. . . . Whether as imperialist or pacifist in tendency; whether to bring to the world peace or a sword; whether inspired by selfish motives of gain or altruistic sentiments of humanity was not so significant in the general growth of American thought as the fundamental fact that the international instinct and interest awoke, and that internationalism won its way against the historic traditions of "splendid isolation."[36]

The Spanish-American War was the most dramatic event in launching the United States upon this course which, as early as 1901, the English journalist W. T. Stead called "the Americanization of the world." Certainly it seemed true that once United States expansion abroad had reached the point where the country was willing to assume the task of governing overseas dependencies, it was less difficult to take the next portentous step and embark upon an international crusade for peace and democracy.

SELECTED REFERENCES

Beale, Howard K. *Theodore Roosevelt and the Rise of America to World Power*. Baltimore: Johns Hopkins Press, 1956.

[35] Annual Message, December 6, 1904, in *Foreign Relations 1904* (Washington, 1905), xli.

[36] C. E. Merriam, *American Political Ideas* (New York, 1929), 253–254.

Davis, George T. *A Navy Second to None: The Development of Modern American Naval Policy.* New York: Harcourt, Brace, 1940.

Dulles, Foster R. *America's Rise to World Power, 1898–1954.* New York: Harper, 1955.

Griswold, A. Whitney. *The Far Eastern Policy of the United States.* New Haven: Yale University Press, 1962.

Harrington, F. H. "The Anti-Imperialist Movement in the United States, 1898–1900," *Mississippi Valley Historical Review,* XXII (September, 1935), 211–230.

———. "Literary Aspects of American Anti-Imperialism, 1898–1902," *New England Quarterly,* X (December, 1937), 650–667.

La Feber, Walter. *The New Empire: An Interpretation of American Expansion, 1860–1898.* Ithaca, N.Y.: Cornell University Press, 1963.

May, Ernest R. *Imperial Democracy: The Emergence of America As a Great Power.* New York: Harcourt, Brace & World, 1961.

Nearing, Scott and Joseph Freeman. *Dollar Diplomacy: A Study in American Imperialism.* New York: Huebsch & Viking Press, 1926.

Pratt, Julius W. *America's Colonial Experiment.* New York: Prentice-Hall, 1950.

———. *Expansionists of 1898: The Acquisition of Hawaii and the Spanish Islands.* Baltimore: Johns Hopkins Press, 1936.

VI

For Peace and Democracy

The early years of the twentieth century, before the outbreak of the First World War, was an era in which men's visions of peace and democracy had seldom, if ever, appeared brighter. In spite of the rival systems of alliances in Europe and such instances of imperialist strife as the Spanish-American, Boer, and Russo-Japanese Wars, the major world powers seemed to have achieved in large measure a form of international concert or balance. The two Hague Conferences and the several occasions in which the threat of war was successfully averted buoyed popular confidence in the prospects of world peace despite the continued imperialism, militarism, and navalism of the great nations. In a sense the very magnitude of the preparations for war made the idea of its possibility all the more unthinkable. "The Great Illusion," Norman Angell called it in his popular pacifist book published in 1910. And, at the same time, the extension of the suffrage and adoption of social reforms in a number of European countries hopefully provided an added democratic assurance that the voice of the people would be heard, and that it would be raised as never before against all war.

The forces of peace and democracy, growing in Europe, were even stronger in the United States. An American climate of opinion hostile to militarism and imperialism gradually succeeded the martial spirit of the War with Spain. And, though there were certain close ties between the progressive mood of the 1900's and imperialism, it was also true that, in America as in Europe, the progress of democracy and reform suggested that major wars belonged only to the past. Ideals of peace, formerly linked with isolationism in the United States, now became an integral part of an expanded concept of American diplomacy. Moreover, the increasingly interventionist cast of United States foreign policy, reminiscent of the old idea of mission, illustrated anew the determination of many Americans to encourage the worldwide spread of democracy. Thus the goals of peace and democracy, which had never been absent in American foreign policy, became in the twentieth century even more important components of that policy. It was, nevertheless, part of the essential tragedy of American diplomacy that these goals, however close they seemed to be, should still prove so elusive and that war and disillusionment, rather than peace and democracy, should become the major fruits of America's efforts.

Questions of peace or war and of the fate of democratic governments in the world at large took on a new urgency in American foreign policy after 1898. Concepts of mission and manifest destiny had now been made more concrete by imperialism. Having forced a sudden and dramatic entrance upon the stage of world politics, the United States showed a greater concern with the conduct of international affairs. Although moving belatedly to join the European imperialist scramble for markets and colonies, the United States in general was committed to the preservation of peace and the status quo among the powers. Via a diplomatic rapprochement with Great Britain, signalized in the events at the turn of the century, the United States shared the task of helping to conserve the existing international structure. For the Far East in 1899, John Hay suggested the Open Door policy as a means of furthering American trade and of averting the dismemberment of the Chinese Empire. Subsequently the net effect of Theodore Roosevelt's interventionist and aggressive diplomacy was the maintenance of the strong United States position in Latin America and the continuance of the precarious balance of power among the nations in the Far East and Europe.

Like the other great powers, the United States in its foreign policy could not escape many of the economic and political pressures that caused a good deal of national inconsistency. Along with the pursuit of ideals of peace and democracy, for example, went involvement in war and power politics and the paradox of a growing peace movement in the midst of mounting appropriations for armaments and battleships. The peace and order, security and military power, which had formerly been taken for granted in the isolated

America of the nineteenth century now became matters of more conscious choice and positive national policy. For virtually the first time in its history, except in war, the United States took seriously the establishment of a strong military force. At the same time the peace which had largely been assumed in the course of a century of political separation from the strife of Europe, suddenly seemed to require the attention, and even participation, of the United States as a member of the several international conferences that were convened in the early 1900's. Exercising its new-found powers America moved toward world leadership, intervening in the cause of peace and democracy and urging the view that peace must be enforced, if necessary—through what was certainly the ultimate paradox—by war. In this fashion, in a period of only some twenty years, a foreign policy that had been formulated to free Cuba was transfigured, via the Philippines and the Far East and then the Great European War, into a holy crusade to make the world safe for peace and democracy. For such a task the American people felt themselves equipped not only by history but also by the foreign policies asserted in the era from McKinley to Wilson.

The physical and military security which the United States had traditionally enjoyed contributed to the American image of an innocent and peace-loving nation. Throughout most of the nineteenth century the United States had been safe from the dangers of hostile attack or invasion. As C. Vann Woodward has pointed out, "This security was not only remarkably effective, but it was relatively free. . . . Between the second war with England and World War II, the United States was blessed with a security so complete and so free that it was able virtually to do without an army and for the greater part of the period without a navy as well." [1] At home neither the Canadian nor the Mexican boundary lines required expensive fortifications, and the few thousand men in the United States army were mostly scattered in outposts along the Indian frontier in the West. Overseas the American merchant marine benefited from the peace which the British navy enforced through-

[1] C. V. Woodward, "The Age of Reinterpretation," *American Historical Review*, LXVI (October, 1960), 2–3.

out much of the world. And, except in wartime, United States annual expenditures for military purposes rarely came to as much as one percent of the gross national product, while less than one percent of the potential military manpower of the country experienced actual service.

This aversion to a large military establishment and devotion to peace was a part of the historical tradition of American foreign policy. The provisions of the Constitution and the inclinations of the Founding Fathers were alike hostile to any evidences of militarism, while peace and isolation from the strife of Europe were an ever-present concern of early American diplomacy. Despite their recurrent skirmishes with the Indian tribes and the violence and lawlessness which characterized parts of the Western frontier, the American people regarded themselves as friendly and pacific in disposition. Although the Mexican War and the Civil War were hardly compatible with this self-image, the broad ideal of peace as a goal of American foreign policy survived, and organized peace societies again attracted the attention of reformers and won a measure of popular backing and national influence in the years after 1865. The War with Mexico came to be looked upon in these circles as a national aberration, while the Civil War in overthrowing the great wrong of slavery did not, it was pointed out, involve the nation in a foreign conflict. Even the brief struggle with Spain was begun as a humanitarian crusade to free Cuba and, despite the ensuing imperialism and fighting in the Philippines, it did not seriously undermine American self-confidence in the picture of the United States as a peace-loving nation.

To square image and reality is never an easy task, whether for nations or individuals. In a sense the history of United States diplomacy in the twentieth century revolves around this problem as the American people have attempted to reconcile the changing position of the United States with the older ideals and interests that traditionally shaped the course of American foreign policy. Although it seems obvious today that the problems and conditions of foreign affairs in the twentieth century differ widely from those of the nineteenth, the break in the continuity of history is seldom complete or clearly defined. Despite the general correctness of the view that the years at the turn of the century marked a major shift in American foreign policy, that policy continued to be affected

by the ideas of the past. Imperialism, intervention, and internationalism did not overcome all at once the isolationist beliefs of
large parts of the American public. And both the Spanish-American
War and the First World War were followed by certain strong,
isolationist reactions in popular feeling.

Yet, on balance, there was a change. Values formerly taken for
granted no longer operated automatically. The sense of national
security and of confidence in the peaceful progress of American
institutions became, if not less certain, at least less carefree. If it
was true that the United States emerged at this stage in its history
a great power as well as a great nation, it was no less true that the
transition involved a heavy price in terms of responsibility and costs.
Thus, in the period from the turn of the century to American entrance into the First World War, there can be discerned the beginnings of a major shift in the thinking about American foreign
policy. Without yielding their faith in the goals of peace and democracy as mainsprings of that policy, the American people became
more willing to accept new means to accomplish these ends. The
methods of peace through power, and of democracy by intervention
and force rather than by example, though not without precedent in
American history, came to achieve nevertheless a new degree of
official sanction and popular support. Imperialism and the passing
of a century of relative security meant that military considerations
would play an increasingly important part in foreign affairs. And,
involvement in world politics now also entailed sending American
soldiers and sailors as well as missionaries and traders to the far
corners of the world.

A prominent feature of the developing foreign policy of the
United States in the twentieth century was a new conception of
military and naval power. In place of the historic reliance on small
defensive forces composed largely of volunteers, the United States
began to pattern its military establishment on the model of the
professional armies and navies in Europe. The modern American
navy had already begun to take form as early as the 1880's and '90's,
and the ideas of Mahan had helped to spread the gospel of navalism
abroad as well as at home. The growing European naval building,

which Mahan's writings did a good deal to encourage, stimulated, in turn, demands for additional construction in the United States, and America also followed the European powers in the creation of a professional staff or board of naval experts dedicated to preparing the blueprints for future wars. As an imperial and naval power America could no longer think primarily in terms of defense. War overseas, at least in the mind of American naval officers, was too likely a possibility to go unplanned or to be left in matters of detail to the vagaries of partisan politics.

By the time of the War with Spain, the American navy had become not only a formidable fighting force but also a professional establishment influential within the counsels of government and business. Through their advice on matters of strategy, senior naval officers were able to affect American diplomacy, and naval construction itself now became an important economic interest of American industry and labor. It was not surprising, accordingly, that Captain, later Admiral, Mahan was sent as one of the American delegates to the First Hague Conference in 1899. At the Conference Mahan, a staunch believer in the philosophy that vital national interests should never be compromised or arbitrated, stated that the United States was not prepared to discuss the question of any limitation of armaments.

At this time the cause of a big navy also received the backing of the newly founded Navy League of the United States. Modeled after similar societies in Europe, the League united the various interest groups in the United States which were working to encourage effective naval legislation. Though never a large organization in terms of its budget or membership, it included an elite of retired naval officers, businessmen, and industrialists, with former statesmen and top-ranking munitions manufacturers as its honorary officials. In matters of foreign and naval policy, the League's views carried weight with both Congress and the general public and, in the opinion of a leading scholar, were "unquestionably a factor of no small importance in the remarkable success with which President Roosevelt brought about an increase of naval power, unapproached in any previous comparable period in American history." [2]

2 Harold and Margaret Sprout, *The Rise of American Naval Power* (Princeton, 1939), 258. For a differing view, see Armin Rappaport, *The Navy League of the United States* (Detroit, 1962).

Traditionally the first line of defense, the navy in the twentieth century became as well a powerful battle fleet organized for offensive action on the high seas. Since defense of the continental United States was not a real problem, the historic concept of the navy's role was widened to include the protection of colonies and bases overseas. The original meaning of defense, under the impact of imperialism and world politics, had been strained to the bursting point. But the popular image was still a useful adjunct to cover aggressive operations in the Caribbean and the Pacific and to forestall the mounting popular and pacifist criticism of a big navy during the later Theodore Roosevelt and Taft Administrations.

Even more than in the case of the navy, the early 1900's marked a revolution in the development of the army. While a large navy had always commanded considerable public support in the United States, an extensive standing army had always been associated in the American mind with European despotism and militarism. Traditionally the citizen soldier served only in time of war, and the small American peacetime regular army of the nineteenth century had been little more than a constabulary used to fight the Indians and to quell domestic disturbances. Thus the reorganization of the army following the War with Spain was an especially significant part of the revolution in military thinking which accompanied the new American diplomacy.

The logistical problems of the War Department, at the outset of the conflict with Spain in 1898, opened the way for the organizational reforms pushed through Congress under the leadership of the new Secretary of War Elihu Root. The army, in view of its traditionally limited role, was ill-prepared for the Spanish-American War and overseas duty, but the country, sparked by the criticisms of Roosevelt and his friends, was ready for drastic measures. While Secretary Root accepted it as a truism that "the real object of having an army is to provide for war," [3] this had by no means been the army's major function throughout most of American history. In any case it was largely Root, a military-minded civilian lawyer, who pressured a reluctant Congress to pass legislation in 1903 transforming the state militia into a federalized National Guard and establishing a professional General Staff. Root, more than anyone, became the architect of the new spirit of militarism which developed

[3] Elihu Root, *Five Years of the War Department* (Washington, 1904), 58.

in the United States in the 1900's and, as Walter Millis has written, it was he who in large part "brought the military managerial revolution to the United States. The German General Staff was admittedly his model; even if Root did not see it, the conscript mass army, available for aggressive action upon a world stage, was the logical end." [4] This new General Staff, especially under General Leonard Wood in Taft's Presidency, became an important lobbying agent, urging greater military preparedness upon Congress as backing for a stronger foreign policy. In a similar way Root himself thought of the reorganized militia or National Guard as a force for "the creation of the military spirit among the youth of the country, to the education and training of that military spirit. . . ." [5]

The Root-Wood variety of militarism, plus the already well-developed navalism in the United States, was at least indirectly a factor in the support of a more ambitious foreign policy. Together with the expanding economic forces of an industrial economy, this militarism and navalism furnished the material foundation for much of the aggressive interventionist American diplomacy of the Roosevelt, Taft, and Wilson Administrations. It was no accident, therefore, that it was Root who had earlier drafted the Platt Amendment, governing American relations with Cuba and turning the island into a virtual protectorate of the United States. It was also fitting that, in Roosevelt's second Administration, Root should succeed John Hay as Secretary of State, symbolizing by his transfer from the War Department the growing interrelations of American foreign and military policies.

Keeping pace with the strategic importance of military and naval affairs in foreign policy was the rising popular support for the peace movement in the United States. Although this juxtaposition of pacifism and militarism, as opposing influences upon American foreign policy, seems at first glance an obvious paradox, there is nevertheless a certain logic in the fact that, as the world in the 1900's

4 Walter Millis, *Arms and Men* (New York, 1956), 180.

5 Elihu Root, *The Military and Colonial Policy of the United States* (Cambridge, Mass., 1916), 147.

moved toward either a more permanent peace or more frightful war, the opposite poles of thought in diplomacy should also be strengthened. Thus the peace movement in the United States in the decade before the First World War alternated between fears of a coming war and hopes that such a catastrophe could, after all, be averted. It was especially ironic that this period in the history of the peace movement, which has been termed "Toward Victory," should also have been the one that was climaxed by the first general war since 1815.

During these last years before 1914 the peace movement suddenly became not only respectable but even fashionable and popular. In contrast to the limited support won by the older peace societies in the nineteenth century and the general lack of success which characterized the anti-imperialist movement at the turn of the century, the peace cause now began to command widespread public approval. Via arbitration through the Hague Tribunal or by the bilateral treaties which received the nonpartisan backing of Elihu Root, President Taft, and William Jennings Bryan, peace no longer seemed a Utopian dream but a practical political and international possibility. Statesmen and wealthy philanthropists gave their time and money, while the crusade against war, formerly associated with a religious pacifism or radical socialism, became political and businesslike. Some of the peace organizations were endowed with substantial funds as individuals like Andrew Carnegie and Edward Ginn contributed generously. Carnegie himself was chosen president of the New York Peace Society, which included on its rolls the flower of the New York City elite, with financiers from Wall Street as well as prominent clergymen participating as members. Special peace societies were established to work with youth in the schools and colleges and to counter the militarist arguments for preparedness and universal military training.

This new-found popularity of peace was reflected in Congress. Even though peace in the sense of international arbitration and mediation remained a complex matter in its relations to national ambitions and interests, there seemed to be gains. Members of the House and Senate, spurred by peace petitions and the lobbying of pacifist groups, gave increasing approval to the idea of international arbitration and disarmament, and at the same time stronger Congressional opposition greeted the annual naval appropriation bills, forcing cuts and modifications in the original Roosevelt building program. Commercial and financial interests, in turn, backed Congressmen in the argument that international trade was a better agent of peace than battleships.

In the White House peace also won qualified support. President Roosevelt, with all his bellicosity and stress on military preparedness, helped to dramatize the peace cause by winning the Nobel Prize in 1906. Taft, his successor, despite his aggressive pursuit of American commercial interests abroad via his so-called dollar diplomacy, was pacific in disposition and intent. His administration, he reported to Congress, in its diplomatic endeavors

has sought to respond to modern ideas of commercial intercourse. This policy has been characterized as substituting dollars for bullets. It is one that appeals alike to idealistic and humanitarian sentiments, to the dictates of sound policy and strategy, and to legitimate commercial aims. It is an effort frankly directed to the increase of American trade upon the axiomatic principle that the Government of the United States shall extend all proper support to every legitimate and beneficial American enterprise abroad.[6]

Although Woodrow Wilson was not a doctrinaire pacifist, he looked upon war and violence as the supreme folly of mankind. Enrolled as a member of the American Peace Society, the oldest such organization in the United States, he gained the votes of some of the Progressives who were repelled by Roosevelt's militarism.

Wilson, it should be noted, espoused a new positive conception of peace as a part of the American mission. As early as 1902, while still a minor prophet confined to the academic world, Wilson, believing that the United States had achieved full maturity and that the day of isolation was past, affirmed: "A new age is before us in which, it would seem, we must lead the world." Nor, despite his peace convictions, did the future President rule out a holy war. In an address in 1911, he noted that "there are times in the history of nations when they must take up the instruments of bloodshed in order to vindicate spiritual conceptions. For liberty is a spiritual conception, and when men take up arms to set other men free, there is something sacred and holy in the warfare. I will not cry

[6] Annual Message, December 3, 1912, in *Papers Relating to the Foreign Relations of the United States, 1912* (Washington, 1919), x.

'peace,' " Wilson added, "so long as there is sin and wrong in the world." [7]

As President, Wilson's idealistic, moralistic conceptions of peace and democracy involved his administration in strange contradictions. No sooner had he pronounced in his Mobile Address the reversal of his predecessors' policies of dollar diplomacy and armed intervention in Latin America, than a series of incidents led to the dispatch of United States troops to Mexico. The criticism of paternalistic imperialism implied in his statement that his administration had "no sympathy with those who seek to seize the power of government to advance their own personal interests or ambition," was interpreted to indicate his own hostility toward the Huerta revolutionary regime in Mexico.[8] By refusing to recognize this Mexican Government, which he believed had gained power by unconstitutional and undemocratic means, Wilson also reversed the well-established United States tradition of being willing to enter into diplomatic relations with any government which, in fact, was able to maintain itself in authority. In actual practice it was apparent that Wilson's diplomacy in Latin America represented no real change from the aggressive economic and military program carried out by Presidents Roosevelt and Taft. But the contrast between Wilson's ideals and his conduct of American foreign policy underscored the dilemma of a world which in 1914 espoused both peace and war, imperialism and democracy, apparently without awareness of inconsistency or contradiction in its beliefs and values.

The outbreak of the Great War in Europe, though not unexpected in diplomatic circles, came as a surprise to the American people. At first the general reaction in the United States was to strengthen popular isolationist feelings, reinforcing the idea of America as a bastion of peace in contrast to a war-torn Europe. The historian Albert Bushnell Hart, whose hastily written book, *The*

[7] *Public Papers of Woodrow Wilson,* R. S. Baker and W. E. Dodd, eds. (New York, 1925–1927), I, 461, II, 294.

[8] R. S. Baker, *Woodrow Wilson: Life and Letters* (Garden City, N.Y., 1927–1939), IV, 66ff.

War In Europe Its Causes and Results, was published in the fall of 1914, reflected a widespread American view that the holocaust had come as a result of European militarism and the mounting armaments race of the preceding years. Although there was no question of the United States' own declaration of a formal neutrality, President Wilson felt it necessary to admonish the American people to "be impartial in thought as well as action." The President also questioned the growing pressures upon Congress, which the hostilities in Europe encouraged, for greater military and naval spending. In his annual message in December, 1914, in reply to Theodore Roosevelt and other Republican critics of his neutrality policy, Wilson made the point that the involvement of the major European powers in the war made it less likely that they could interfere in the affairs of the New World and thus lessened any immediate threat to the security of the United States.

These initial sentiments of isolation, peace, and neutrality, though rooted in American traditions, soon began to lose their decisive character as mainsprings in the conduct of American diplomacy. From the outset it was clear that despite all injunctions of neutrality in thought and action, American sympathies lay with England and France, against Germany. At the same time the Atlantic Ocean quickly became the avenue of a burgeoning wartime trade which was almost entirely confined to the Allied Powers. When German submarines attempted to break the British blockade, important questions of neutral rights on the high seas were raised on which the Wilson administration was not disposed to yield, especially in the case of their violation by the German Empire.

In this insistence on the maritime rights of the United States as a neutral to send its farm products and manufactures across the Atlantic to the Allies without interference by German submarines, the Wilson Administration was in practice jeopardizing the very neutrality which it in theory maintained. Though correct in a technical and legal sense, the Administration's position ran the danger of sacrificing the substance of neutrality and of identifying the national honor of the United States with procedural matters which, however traditional, were also becoming outmoded. To a later generation this American concern over neutral rights would seem unrealistic, but at the time neither the public nor the Administration was willing to pay the price of peace and neutrality if it entailed cutting off the American economy from the war in Europe through a self-denying embargo on the export of munitions and raw materials.

When President Wilson in 1915, still hopeful of peace despite the practical American abandonment of isolation and a realistic neutrality, refused to follow the counsel of his more belligerent advisors and urge United States entrance into the war, his hesitation seemed to many of his political opponents an indication of weakness. Partly to forestall these critics, the President reversed his original stand that large-scale American military spending was unnecessary and became a strong proponent of preparedness legislation. In his campaign for reelection in 1916 Wilson, accepting both preparedness and the slogan "He Kept Us Out of War," reflected popular if ambivalent American anxieties. What the public wanted was a foreign and military policy strong enough to defend the United States and keep the country out of war. What the general population could hardly understand, however, was that Wilson's diplomacy had already carried the nation to the brink of war and that the larger army and navy for which the Congress voted was being raised not for the defense of the continental United States but for service overseas.

More clearsighted, or more frank, than most of Wilson's supporters, Herbert Croly, editor of the liberal *New Republic* magazine, announced that he backed the preparedness program despite its violation of American antimilitarist traditions, because of the danger that America would soon become involved in the war. "The usual explanation that the United States is preparing only for defense, which is a policy on which all good citizens can agree, merely begs the question," Croly asserted. In the case of a major power like the United States, "no sharp line can be drawn between defensive and aggressive armament." Thus in Croly's view the "dubious aspect" of preparedness lay not in its cost, but "in the ambiguity of its underlying purpose." He was also willing to admit that "there is a very real probability that the new Army and Navy will be used chiefly for positive and aggressive as opposed to merely defensive purposes." [9]

[9] Herbert Croly, "The Effect on American Institutions of a Powerful Military and Naval Establishment," *Annals of the American Academy of Political and Social Science*, XVI (July, 1916), 157–172.

Croly's analysis of the underlying rationale of the Wilson military policy was much the same as that of Wilson's pacifist critics; it
moved, however, to a different conclusion than theirs—to American
belligerency rather than continued neutrality. To Croly, United
States entrance in the war was in keeping with the realistic version
of progressive political theory which he had offered a few years back
in his *The Promise of American Life*. Despite the progress of
democracy and reform in much of Europe, Croly perceived that
the Continent was basically organized for war. "The nations of
Europe," he wrote in 1910, "are to all appearances as belligerent as
were the former dynastic states. Europe has become a vast camp,
and its governments are spending probably a larger proportion of
the resources of their countries for military and naval purposes than
did those of the eighteenth century." [10]

In this organization for aggressive war lay the basic antagonism
between the European and the American political systems. This was
the foundation of the American isolationism which, Croly believed,
had been the correct policy of the United States in the nineteenth
century. The sincerity of the continued American professions of
peace, he suggested, must be manifested in the building of a strong
and stable international system for the two American continents.
The chief obstacle to achieving this kind of a stable American system lay in the domestic disorders characteristic of some of the Latin
American states. "Just what can be done with such states is a knotty
problem," Croly conceded, and he accepted therefore the doctrine
of American intervention. "In all probability," he concluded, "no
American international system will ever be established without the
forcible pacification of one or more such centers of disorder." [11]

Just as Croly predicted the course of Wilson's Latin American
policy and Mexican intervention, so he also, like Wilson, moved to
the next step of United States intervention in Europe in the cause of
world peace and democracy. Croly was aware that the notion of
American involvement in a European conflict violated an "absolute
law—derived from the sacred writings" on American foreign policy.
The prospect of such a war, he wrote in 1910, "would at present be
received with pious horror by the great majority of Americans." Yet,
in Croly's mind, the American desire for peace which in the past

10 Herbert Croly, *The Promise of American Life* (New York, 1910), 254.
11 *Ibid.*, 302.

had constituted the chief justification for national isolation might at some later date require American intervention and war.

The American responsibility in this respect is similar to that of any peace-preferring European Power. If it wants peace, it must be spiritually and physically prepared to fight for it. Peace will prevail in international relations, just as order prevails within a nation, because of the righteous use of superior force—because the power which makes for pacific organization is stronger than the power which makes for a warlike organization. It looks as if at some future time the power of the United States might well be sufficient, when thrown into the balance, to tip the scales in favor of a comparatively pacific settlement of international complications. Under such conditions a policy of neutrality would be a policy of irresponsibility and unwisdom.[12]

To President Wilson, torn between his desire for peace and his fears of the eventual necessity of intervention, the concept of a peace enforced by American arms was Heaven-sent. To a remarkable degree Wilson's life and training, from his Calvinist upbringing through his career in teaching and politics, had been a preparation for this idea of a new American mission. The armed intervention which he carried out in Mexico and the Caribbean served as a prelude to an American expeditionary force in France. At the same time, it now seemed logical that United States assumptions of responsibility for international order in one hemisphere should be extended to the other. "We regard war," the President informed the Congress in December, 1915, "merely as a means of asserting the rights of a people against aggression." [13]

Finally American entrance into the war in April, 1917, raised the possibility that the ideals of progressive democracy, carried forward at home under the banner of the New Freedom, might resuscitate a war-torn and reactionary Europe. According to John Dewey, whose own wartime philosophy was a curious mixture of pragmatism and idealism, America, in joining the European war belatedly, would have to do what it could to see that its ideals were "forced upon our allies, however unwilling they may be, rather than [be] covered up by the débris of war." [14] In the words of

[12] *Ibid.*, 312.

[13] *Public Papers of Woodrow Wilson*, III, 411.

[14] John Dewey, "The Future of Pacifism," *New Republic*, XI (July 28, 1917), 359.

Richard Hofstadter, "the wartime frenzy of idealism and self-sacrifice marked the apotheosis as well as the liquidation of the Progressive spirit." [15] Thus it was clear that in the long run the missionary note of a positive and militant American world leadership was far more persuasive in Wilson's thinking about foreign policy than any traditional concepts of a liberal pacifism or a neutral isolationism.

As he took the last fateful steps leading to the American declaration of war, Wilson was comforted by visions of the kind of postwar world suggested in the program of the League to Enforce Peace. The varied pieces in the Wilsonian foreign policy were gradually falling into place as the inner contradictions of peace and war, preparedness and neutrality, isolation and intervention, were all reconciled in the concept of a crusade for peace and democracy with the goal of a league of nations to make good the terms of the postwar settlement. In place of a limited peace, "a peace without victory," mediated with the help of a neutral United States and continuing the European balance of power, American belligerency implied total victory and a war to the Utopian end of a new democratic and international association of the world's nations. In the name of such principles, Wilson could ask the peoples of the United States and the Allies to fight in what in his own mind was essentially a holy war—an unprecedented kind of secular crusade for the future of all mankind.

Carried into the War on a wave of emotional idealism, and believing their national honor affronted by the German submarines, the American people nevertheless had no clear understanding of the struggle in terms of national self-interest. In relation to America's historic isolationist and neutralist traditions and to the nation's pacific ideals, the war involved a sharp break with the past which only the overriding emphasis on victory and Wilson's rhetoric of peace and democracy were able to reconcile. Essentially, however, there was a gulf between Wilson's lofty ideals and the more prosaic

[15] Richard Hofstadter, *The Age of Reform* (New York, 1955), 273.

desires of the American people. While the President thought of the war in terms of his future goals, the American people went to war because they were not willing to forego the material advantages which a program of isolated neutrality would have required. The American public, despite the patriotic enthusiasm generated by the coming of the War, was not ready, for example, to accept the struggle in terms of Wilson's War Message, and this fact became of increasing significance in understanding the fate of the President's plans for peacemaking and the League of Nations.

Before the War, in the midst of numerous vague and informal suggestions looking toward some sort of international organization, Herbert Croly had made the point that, if the United States accepted the invitation to join such a body, it should be on the basis of a sound and well-informed conception of national interest. This task of convincing the American public that it was in the interest of the United States to abandon its long-standing policies of isolation and neutrality for a version of collective security was assumed by President Wilson even before America entered the War. On May 27, 1916, before the League to Enforce Peace, the President made an address which Harley Notter called the "most important pronouncement on American policy since 1823." [16] As spokesman of the American Government, Wilson believed that he should attempt to express the thought and purpose of the people of the United States regarding a war in which "our own rights as a Nation, the liberties, the privileges, and the property of our people have been profoundly affected." Not only did the American people desire to see the War concluded but, in addition, Wilson declared,

when it does come to an end we shall be as much concerned as the nations at war to see peace assume an aspect of permanence, give promise of days from which the anxiety of uncertainty shall be lifted, bring some assurance that peace and war shall always hereafter be reckoned part of the common interest of mankind. We are participants, whether we would or not, in the life of the world. The interests of all nations are our own also. We are partners with the rest. What affects mankind is inevitably our affair as well as the affair of the nations of Europe and of Asia.[17]

[16] Harley Notter, *The Origins of the Foreign Policy of Woodrow Wilson* (Baltimore, 1937), 521.

[17] *Public Papers of Woodrow Wilson,* IV, 184–185.

Although as an historian Wilson recognized that wars sprang from economic competition as well as from political injustice, he was primarily concerned that there be some international mechanism in which the force of world public opinion could deter the force of national aggression. Blaming the secret diplomacy of the powers as a major cause of the War, Wilson felt it was clear that "the peace of the world must henceforth depend upon a new and more wholesome diplomacy." First, every people must have the right to choose their sovereignty. Second, small states must have rights equivalent to those of large states. And third, the world has a right to be free from wars of aggression. "So sincerely do we believe in these things," the President concluded, "that I am sure that I speak the mind and wish of the people of America when I say that the United States is willing to become a partner in any feasible association of nations formed in order to realize these objects and make them secure against violation." [18]

Until the United States became a belligerent, the President could not speak out freely on the subject of the specific territorial readjustments which he believed were needed among the nations, but in his address to the Senate on January 22, 1917, he asserted that it was inconceivable that the people of the United States should play no part in the peacemaking. And the terms of that peace, Wilson emphasized, implied "first of all, that it must be a peace without victory," a peace founded on an equality of rights among nations and upon "the principle that governments derive all their just powers from the consent of the governed. . . ." [19] Stability within nations and among nations would be further secured by a program of disarmament and by the insurance of freedom of the seas.

Democracy, in the sense of the self-determination of nations and the popular consent of the governed, the President made it clear, was an essential condition of a workable peace. In his concern with the internal stability of nations along with their international harmony, Wilson adhered to his belief that the foreign and domestic policies of a country could not be separated. Thus, in his mind, peace and democracy were linked as related goals in the American

18 *Ibid.*, IV, 185–187.
19 *Ibid.*, IV, 410–411.

foreign policy for which he attempted to gain support both at home and abroad. It was more than the mere rhetoric called for by the occasion, therefore, which led the President in his War Message to urge his fellow Americans to fight "for the ultimate peace of the world and for the liberation of its peoples. . . ." In asserting his famous plea, "The world must be made safe for democracy," the President explained:

A steadfast concert for peace can never be maintained except by a partnership of democratic nations. No autocratic government could be trusted to keep faith within it or observe its covenants. It must be a league of honor, a partnership of opinion. Intrigue would eat its vitals away; the plottings of inner circles who could plan what they would and render account to no one would be a corruption seated at its very heart. Only free peoples can hold their purpose and their honor steady to a common end and prefer the interests of mankind to any narrow interest of their own.[20]

In his program for the future peace of the world, Wilson stressed the importance of political justice and an international concert enforced through the joint powers of public opinion and an association of nations. In a world so organized, he believed, national economic competition would not lead to political aggression, while law and order would be maintained without the heavy burden of large armies and navies. Spelling out his conditions for permanent peace in more detail after America had entered the War, Wilson included as the last of the famous Fourteen Points his proposal that "A general association of nations must be formed under specific covenants for the purpose of affording mutual guarantees of political independence and territorial integrity to great and small states alike." [21]

It is apparent that Wilson's program, as he stated it, was essentially an idealistic and visionary one. It set forth aims with which there could be little basic disagreement; at the same time, however, even though he himself believed that the League of Nations would

20 *Ibid.*, V, 12, 14.
21 *Ibid.*, V. 161.

provide such a mechanism, the program offered little in the way of realistic methods to achieve its idealistic goals. Moreover, as Robert Osgood points out:

> President Wilson's leadership throughout the period of war and peace-making, though it was eternally right in its moral objectives, could not have been deliberately calculated to defeat its own ends more surely; for by exhorting his countrymen to subordinate their self-interest to abstract moral standards and the welfare of the rest of the world, Wilson demanded an impossible and unnecessary performance, encouraged the postwar repudiation of the very objects he sought, and obscured the one basis upon which a more realistic view of national conduct could have been created, a basis which might have recommmended itself to nationalists and inter-nationalists, egoists and idealists alike. That basis was enlightened self-interest.[22]

Actually the Treaty of Versailles was neither as idealistic as President Wilson asserted nor as contrary to American national power and security as its Republican opponents alleged. In sub-mitting the Treaty with the Covenant of the League to the Senate, the President, as Albert Weinberg has noted, "displayed the greatest skill in assimilating to traditional American attitudes this radical departure from isolation." [23] The course of America's expansionist foreign policy since 1898 Wilson interpreted as an abandonment of provincialism and isolation. In the light of this recent past, he urged: "There can be no question of our ceasing to be a world power. The only question is whether we can refuse the moral leadership that is offered us, whether we shall accept or reject the confidence of the world." [24] Essentially, however, the Treaty of Versailles imposed upon Germany what was a victor's peace, in-compatible with the high aims which the President himself had set forth before America entered the war, and again in his Fourteen Points. But the compromises with the Allies that Wilson felt forced to work out at the Paris Peace Conference he rationalized with his faith that the League of Nations would inaugurate a new and revolutionary era in world politics and diplomacy. The League, he

22 R. E. Osgood, *Ideals and Self-Interest in America's Foreign Relations* (Chicago, 1953), 303.

23 A. K. Weinberg, *Manifest Destiny* (Baltimore, 1935), 470.

24 *Public Papers of Woodrow Wilson*, V, 551.

seemed to think, would be able to serve as both the conscience and the policeman of mankind.

Attacked by conservative nationalists like Henry Cabot Lodge and Theodore Roosevelt for sacrificing American interests in behalf of his world vision, Wilson also lost the support of liberals in both the isolationist and internationalist camps because each group, in its own way, felt that the Treaty and the League did not establish a real peace based on the equality and consent of peoples and nations. In the celebrated declaration of disillusionment which the *New Republic* magazine printed on the cover of its first issue after the text of the Treaty arrived in the United States, the editors proclaimed:

THIS IS NOT PEACE. Americans would be fools if they permitted themselves to be embroiled in a system of European alliances. America promised to underwrite a stable peace. Mr. Wilson has failed. The peace cannot last. America should withdraw from all commitments which would impair her freedom of action.[25]

Earlier when the President, at Paris, resorting to realistic diplomacy, used the threat of America's potential naval strength in an attempt to force agreement with some of his ideas, he not only antagonized the idealists but he also offered Senator Lodge the opportunity to remark on the floor of Congress:

. . . it seems to me extraordinary that we should enter on a scheme for eternal peace throughout the world by proposing to build a navy which in seven years is to be equal to that of England. . . . How it fits with the policy of reduction of naval and military forces or with the high objects of a league of nations I can not conceive.[26]

In retrospect it would appear that the American people followed the Senate in its rejection of the Treaty of Versailles because the League of Nations, in particular, represented a radical departure from the traditions of American foreign policy without offering, in turn, any direct compensatory advantages. While Wilson denied that American entrance into the war was motivated by any taint of self-seeking or desire for territories, it is by no means sure that many elements in the United States were not seeking to continue the

[25] *New Republic*, XIX (May 24, 1919), cover page.
[26] December 21, 1918, *Congressional Record*, 65 Cong., 3 Sess., 727.

economic imperialism and dollar diplomacy of the prewar years. Even though the President did not envisage his foreign policies as limiting national economic opportunities abroad, his idealistic phrases and program were susceptible of that conclusion.

Although the Wilsonian diplomacy, climaxed by American participation in the war and near-participation in the League, reversed long-standing traditions of isolation, neutrality, and non-intervention, the failure of the United States to join the League did not mean that the American people repudiated historic ideals of peace and democracy. Even some of the irreconcilables who fought the League so bitterly—Senators Norris and La Follette, for example —were among the staunchest advocates of an international understanding based on world disarmament and mutual conciliation. Wilson himself, despite his Cassandra-like warnings of the fate in store for the world if America rejected the League, continued to identify the destiny of the United States with the principles of right and justice which he had asserted during the war. The American people also, though they failed to back Wilson's peacemaking, demonstrated anew in the postwar years their support of the search for peace and democracy as long-range goals of American foreign policy.

SELECTED REFERENCES

Bailey, Thomas A. *Woodrow Wilson and the Lost Peace*. New York: Macmillan, 1944.

———. *Woodrow Wilson and the Great Betrayal*. New York: Macmillan, 1945.

Buehrig, Edward H. *Woodrow Wilson and the Balance of Power*. Bloomington: Indiana University Press, 1955.

Curti, Merle. *Peace or War: The American Struggle, 1636–1936*. New York: Norton, 1936.

Ekirch, Arthur A. *The Civilian and the Military*. New York: Oxford University Press, 1956.

Link, Arthur S. *Wilson the Diplomatist: A Look at His Major Foreign Policies*. Baltimore: Johns Hopkins Press, 1957.

Millis, Walter. *Arms and Men: A Study in American Military History*. New York: Putnam, 1956.

————. *Road to War: America, 1914–1917*. Boston: Houghton Mifflin, 1935.

Notter, Harley F. *The Origins of the Foreign Policy of Woodrow Wilson*. Baltimore: Johns Hopkins Press, 1937.

Tansill, Charles C. *America Goes to War*. Boston: Little, Brown, 1938.

VII

The Renunciation of War

The great crusade for peace and democracy came to a close in 1918 in an atmosphere of increasing disillusionment. The elaborate American experiment of a world mission under arms was soon to be widely regarded as simply a horrible mistake. The renunciation of war—not just the recent World War, but all war—became the dominating influence in the foreign policy of the United States. The American people, though traditionally hostile to militarism, had never before in their history rejected the whole experience and possibility of war with such intense emotional and intellectual finality. The recent conflict, it was now clear, had exacted a frightful toll in lives and property. Although the United States lost only 112,000 men from enemy action or disease, figures available after the Armistice showed that in Europe ten million men had been killed outright, while four times that number had died as a direct or indirect result of the war. Net costs of the war and property losses ran into the hundreds of billions of dollars, leaving enormous debts for future generations to try to pay. "Never again" was to be henceforth a promise as well as a slogan.

In the first years after the war a number of young American writers, inspired by their own personal memories of the experience, expressed the utter revulsion and downright disillusionment of Dos Passos' *Three Soldiers,* Cummings' *Enormous Room,* and Stallings' and Anderson's *What Price Glory.* Later Hemingway's *A Farewell to Arms* and the German novelist Erich Remarque's *All Quiet on the Western Front,* and the movie based on his best-selling book, brought to an even larger American audience an appreciation of the horror and futility of war. Much of the spirit of this postwar disillusionment was recalled appropriately by George Kennan in his lectures on *American Diplomacy* after World War II. Quoting from the closing pages of the novel, in which Remarque depicts the war-weariness of a young German veteran home on leave in a military hospital shortly before the Armistice, Kennan noted:

> Now that was World War I. Those of you here who are veterans may say: "Why, that wasn't just World War I. . . . That was any war." [And Kennan continues:] Right you are. And if there was anything special about the first World War, it was only that the thing went on in the same way and in the same places for an awfully long time; there was not much movement, not much adventure, not much hope that anything could happen that would change the whole fortunes of war at any early date. The losses were terrific on both sides. You could practically calculate when your time would come. And it was all so unutterably futile.[1]

The bleak picture of the First World War in all its drab reality, which was such an integral part of the popular novels of the postwar period, was reinforced by the work of a number of revisionist historians and journalists who attacked the official accounts of the coming of the Great Crusade. The way in which wartime propaganda had been used to arouse the public and spur support for the selfish ambitions of the belligerents was revealed with the publication of Philip Gibbs' *Now It Can Be Told* (1920), Arthur Ponsonby's *Falsehood in Wartime* (1928), and Harold Lasswell's *Propaganda Technique in the World War* (1927). Questioning the Allies' thesis of Germany's sole war guilt were such important early books as Harry Elmer Barnes' *The Genesis of the World War* (1926) and Sidney B. Fay's *The Origins of the World War* (1928). Then in *Why We Fought* (1929) and later in the *Road to War* (1935), C. Hartley Grattan, Walter Millis, and other writers emphasized the role of economic ties and Allied propaganda, rather than the German submarine warfare, as basic causes of American entrance into the European conflict.

Also during these postwar years, United States idealism in regard to the recent War as well as American nationalism and patriotism were questioned by the literary school of debunkers and members of that iconoclastic clan of writers which became known as "the lost generation." Much of this antiwar literature and its favor-

---

[1] G. F. Kennan, *American Diplomacy, 1900–1950* (Chicago, 1951), 60–61.

able notice in the pages of the *New Republic, Nation,* and H. L. Mencken's *American Mercury* magazine affected the social and political thinking of the younger generation of college youth and presumably strengthened its popular pacifist convictions. It would be a mistake, however, to conclude that the postwar literature was merely disillusionist or cynical. In the process of attacking war and the nationalism and patriotism which were traditionally invoked to support it, the writers sought what they believed was the higher idealism of peace. "The lost generation, like the revisionists and the other apostles of disillusionment, wanted to restore, not to destroy, America's blunted enthusiasm for the liberal and humanitarian values. All that it intended to destroy were the sentimental illusions and the corruptions of self-interest which had led idealism astray." [2]

In looking back at the two decades between the World Wars, it is perhaps difficult to see a consistent pattern in American foreign policy. But in this era of continuing confusion between the conflicting forces of isolationism or collective security, nationalism or internationalism, one persistent theme stands out. This was the renunciation of war. From the disarmament conferences of the 1920's, through the Kellogg-Briand Pact, to the neutrality legislation of the 1930's, the rejection of war was the underlying note in American diplomacy. To American statesmen and politicians war, especially another World War, seemed certain to lead to depression at home and revolution abroad. Only peace promised prosperity and freedom, or in President Harding's appropriate expression, "normalcy." This desire for normalcy, even more than isolationism, was the key to the popular and official mood in the early twenties. In their disillusionment over the recent War, the American people did not disavow the idealistic goals for which they had fought—peace and democracy. Only the war and the abnormal forces it had unleashed were repudiated. In contrast peace, a peace without en-

2 R. E. Osgood, *Ideals and Self-Interest in America's Foreign Relations* (Chicago, 1953), 319.

tangling alliances or the further risk of war, would insure a return to normality and enable the American people to take up again the former pattern of their lives. Robert Ferrell makes the point that a first assumption of American diplomats in the 1920's was that "the World War was an unnecessary part of European and world history and that, since the war was finished, history could go back to its ordinary and usual course." [3]

In 1919, in the midst of the struggle in the Senate over the Treaty of Versailles, there had been intense and bitter debate over American foreign policy. A year later the Presidential election, it is generally agreed, registered no clear-cut verdict on internationalism or the League of Nations. Yet Harding's decisive victory probably demonstrated as much as anything the hostility of the electorate toward President Wilson and his War policies. And, after the elections Harding's own comment, "the League is dead," in all likelihood did no more than describe the prevailing state of American public opinion. People wanted to forget the war. "The issues of the day were not war and peace but prohibition, jazz, the Ku Klux Klan, the Big Red Scare, Sacco and Vanzetti, the length of skirts, Teapot Dome, the Scopes 'monkey trial,' and Al Capone. Under the pall of widespread apathy toward international matters, the nation gave free rein to its egoistic impulses. The phenomenon of super-patriotism known as One Hundred Percent Americanism—partly a holdover from the war-born zeal for conformity and partly an attempt by conservatives to get back in the saddle—constituted one of the more unseemly movements that rushed into the vacuum left by the dissolution of the Wilsonian issues." [4]

For those Americans who still cared about such things, the news from across the Atlantic was a powerful stimulus to disillusionment. Bolshevism had triumphed in Russia, while the specter of communism threatened the defeated Central Powers and gave added momentum to the diplomacy of hysteria practiced by the Allies. Continued squabbling among the victor powers, and the prospect of more wars or revolutions in a number of countries, reinforced the

[3] R. H. Ferrell, *American Diplomacy in the Great Depression* (New Haven, 1957), 22.

[4] Osgood, *Ideals and Self-Interest*, 311.

popular American image of Europe as a corrupt and worn-out continent.

Because the League seemed at best an imperfect instrument to cope with this time of troubles in Europe and Asia, many observers felt that American membership would only involve the United States in a host of revolutions and boundary disputes. According to Lord Bryce, the respected English author of the classic *American Commonwealth,* there was "lunacy everywhere in Europe now. We all say to one another the war was bad, but this sort of peace is worse. Indeed, what peace is there when Western Asia and Eastern Europe are still in flames?" [5] American commentators reported pessimistically that militarism was again rife in Europe, and in any case it was obvious that the League was unable to enforce a general disarmament upon its members. Already disillusioned by the Treaty of Versailles, American opinion in its hopes for peace was thus further disappointed by the generally deteriorating world situation. Even so cosmopolitan a figure as Herbert Hoover was among those converted to isolationism by the course of events in Europe following the war.

In the eyes of Woodrow Wilson and others of its supporters, the League of Nations was to be the great international instrument to help stabilize the world and enforce the peace. Within the broad outlines of Wilson's ideals and with the general goals of the League, the American people probably had no real quarrel. Indeed, a frequent complaint, at least in liberal circles, was that the Treaty of Versailles failed to measure up to the noble principles enunciated by the American President in the course of the War. The League, however, as its powerful political critics demonstrated, was a departure from historic American conceptions of foreign policy. It conflicted with the desire for normality. Traditionally Americans accepted the idea that war could be eliminated through the development of moral and legal principles and through the power of an enlightened public opinion. Although the League also recognized these potential deterrents, it seemed to place greater stress on the concept of a peace enforced ultimately, and if necessary, by economic sanctions and war. Its famous Article X, pledging all member states to protect each other's territory and political independence

[5] H. A. L. Fisher, *James Bryce* (New York, 1927), II, 253.

from external aggression, accordingly aroused the strictures not only of American nationalists and isolationists but also of some internationalists as well. For example, Robert Lansing, Wilson's wartime Secretary of State, went so far as to say: "I am willing to rely on the pacific spirit of democracies to accomplish the desirable relation between nations, and I do not believe that any League relying upon force or the menace of force can accomplish that purpose, at least for any length of time." [6]

Diplomacy, Americans expected, should devote itself to abolishing war. Peace and normalcy were the goals of American foreign policy, and rejection of the League of Nations opened the way for the reestablishment of legal and moral principles as the best instruments for achieving these ends. "Senators," William E. Borah declared, "you cannot establish peace by force, by repression. . . . We are told that this treaty means peace. . . . But your treaty does not mean peace—far, very far, from it. If we are to judge the future by the past it means war." [7]

No doubt in the minds of large segments of the American public, peace and normalcy indicated not only a return to the less complicated diplomacy of the nineteenth century, but also the repression of all foreign influences—of aliens and immigrants, radicals and dissenters. Yet isolationism, like disillusionment, had its idealistic aspects. "To many Americans," Alexander DeConde has pointed out, "isolation was nothing more than isolation from war. Although manifested in diverse ways, such as antimilitarism, this antiwar element ran through all forms of isolationist dogma, either as an idea or an emotion." [8] A vital part of the older isolationism of the nineteenth century had been a hatred of European war and militarism, and it was clear again in the twenties and thirties that the country wanted a foreign policy that would minimize the risk of political entanglements or the use of armed force. Beginning with Harding and Hughes there was a reassessment of American national interests. Europe was not regarded as an area worth a war, and in the treaties that were ratified at the Washington Conference

[6] Quoted in R. N. Current, "The United States and 'Collective Security,'" in *Isolation and Security*, Alexander DeConde, ed. (Durham, N.C., 1957), 39.

[7] November 19, 1919, *Congressional Record*, 66 Cong., 1 Sess., 8783.

[8] Alexander DeConde, "On Twentieth-Century Isolationism," in *Isolation and Security*, 31.

Hughes made this explicit in regard to Asia. Even in Latin America more and more Americans questioned the wisdom of the United States' traditional policy of military intervention.

Despite the nostalgic isolationism of many Americans, normalcy, in the light of the revolutionary changes brought about by the Great War, was hardly possible. For one thing, the economic power of the United States had grown tremendously. A debtor nation before the war, America was now not only the creditor of Europe but, in addition, America's industrial production and national income almost exceeded that of all other nations combined. In an economic sense the United States was, indeed, the colossus of the Western world. By the 1920's the domestic pressures for economic expansion abroad, growing since at least the late nineteenth century, were again an important influence on American foreign policy. Foreign markets were necessary to keep the domestic economy functioning smoothly, and international peace in turn was vital to foreign trade. As the richest country in the postwar world, America had the responsibility to play a major role in the preservation of world peace and prosperity.

To the postwar generation wars and revolutions were the chief threats to normalcy and thus also to the peace and prosperity Americans wished to enjoy. The danger of further world revolutions, they hoped, might be isolated or contained by a United States policy of refusing diplomatic recognition to Soviet Russia. Thus the nonrecognition policy instituted by President Wilson was continued throughout the twenties in the Republican Administrations of Harding, Coolidge, and Hoover. But this American political isolationism, however strong it was with respect to war and revolution, was only partially a fact in the economic foreign policy of the United States. America, it was true, pushed its tariffs higher and insisted that Europe pay its war debts. Yet, at the same time, in order to encourage a return to international order and prosperity and to help ward off more wars and revolutions, the American government encouraged liberal loans to Germany and the scaling down of German reparations payments.

Conservative business sentiment in the 1920's considered war a harbinger of social unrest and a threat to economic progress. In the words of Herbert Hoover, the American people came out of the First World War "with a huge debt, increased taxes, inflated currency, inflated agriculture, useless factories, . . . demoralized railways and export trade, and with countless other national losses, which will continue for a generation." [9] Antiwar, but far from isolationist, American businessmen desired both normalcy and prosperity. With the help of the State Department and the Department of Commerce, they eagerly sought new overseas markets. And, in a decade in which business values exercised a controlling influence upon American society and government, American foreign policy, not unnaturally, was responsive to business needs. Tariff laws and reciprocity agreements were used to gain advantages for American exports, while the old nineteenth-century spirit of private competition was succeeded by a new era in which American statesmen zealously encouraged business interests. To a considerable extent dollar diplomacy was supplanted by what Herbert Feis called "the diplomacy of the dollar," with private economic interests put forward under the protective shelter of the nation's foreign policy. Especially in Latin America, where half the countries were either the economic or military wards of the Americans to the north, loans and trade were used to advance the political and diplomatic aims of the United States.

One of the unhappy legacies of the First World War which threatened the prospects of peace and prosperity in the 1920's was the continued heavy expense of large national armaments. Business interests as well as peace groups accordingly supported American political leaders in the movement for international disarmament. While naval building had always stimulated some segments of industry, the heavy costs of a postwar naval race threatened to destroy all Republican hopes of cutting taxes and reducing the national debt. More importantly, if the economic and political issues dividing the great powers could be adjusted and if a program of general disarmament could be initiated, a new pacific era might be achieved without resort to the cumbersome machinery of the League. The American people would then be able to enjoy peace and normalcy

[9] Quoted in R. N. Stromberg, "American Business and the Approach of War," *Journal of Economic History*, XIII (Winter, 1953), 62.

as well as political isolation. And, in the world at large, freed from the threat of war and the burden of extensive armaments, a new high level of general prosperity would become a reality, while all nations would be able to climb out of the deep abyss into which they had been plunged in 1914.

The Harding Administration, though studiously ignoring the League of Nations, could not be indifferent to the popular cry for peace. Whatever their reservations over the methods proposed in the Covenant of the League of Nations, Americans were not hostile to the basic underlying purpose of the League to try to free the world from war. And, despite their indifference to Europe, the American people were not happy to have to shoulder the economic burdens of a naval race and continued large armaments. At the same time, it was politically desirable that the United States find some substitute for the League and that it resolve its growing rivalry with Japan in the Pacific. Of the possible courses available to American diplomacy in 1929, a limited international conference called to consider disarmament and the problems of China and the Far East promised the greatest gains with the least danger for the United States. Such a gathering, convened independently of the League of Nations, need not involve the United States in purely European affairs, and it would not require the presence at the conference table of the two major outcast nations—Germany and Russia.

The treaties which came out of the Washington Conference of 1921–1922 were essentially compromises in which all of the signatory nations yielded something. The results of the Conference made possible a period of recuperation from the war and preserved for another decade the status quo in China and the Pacific. All in all, the Conference was a landmark in history—the most rational of all the postwar agreements and the only one to achieve any practical results. Without committing the United States in Europe, it won support for American interests in the Far East and delayed the Japanese advance in China and the Pacific. So long as the Naval Treaty was upheld, the fleets of neither Japan nor the United States had the power to attack each other; the assault on Pearl Harbor was the result of later circumstances. From the point of view of the American people, and indeed for the whole world, the Washington Conference was a promising beginning in the movement for disarmament and the prevention of war. In Secretary of State Hughes' own words, addressed to the closing session of the Conference:

> This Treaty ends, absolutely ends, the race in competition of naval armament. At the same time it leaves the relative security of the great naval powers unimpaired. . . . We are taking perhaps the greatest forward step in history to establish the reign of peace.[10]

Although the American press and public both accepted the results of the Washington Conference enthusiastically, there was some dissent. Big-navy advocates feared that the United States' surrender of potential naval supremacy would be followed by further reductions, while pacifists were dissatisfied with anything less than complete disarmament. The Washington Treaty had, in effect, only limited the battleships of the large powers to their current relative sizes without enforcing a real disarmament. And, as Senator Borah pointed out during the Congressional debate on the Naval Treaty, large armaments still existed on land and sea. But the naval race in battleships had been stopped—at least for a time. Also the danger of war in the Far East, stimulated by the race prejudice and jingoistic pressure of Americans on the West Coast and by United States fears of Japanese interests and ambitions in China, appeared to be averted. Most important of all, the world's hopes for peace, left unfulfilled and uncertain after the First World War, were now restored.

During the 1920's general disarmament continued to be a major goal of American foreign policy. Yet, in spite of the striking popular and diplomatic success of the Washington Conference, the quest for disarmament made little further headway. The Geneva Naval Conference called by President Coolidge in 1927 proved a complete failure. At London three years later, with the strong backing of President Hoover and the English Prime Minister Ramsay MacDonald, some limited agreement was reached in extending the ship categories covered by the Washington Treaty. But in London

[10] Quoted in Harold and Margaret Sprout, *Toward a New Order of Sea Power* (Princeton, 1940), 252.

in 1930, it may be said that the movement for disarmament reached its peak without achieving its goal—except in the sense of enforcing the status quo and preventing an uncontrolled naval race among the great powers. Subsequent conferences, at Geneva in 1932 and at London again in 1935, accomplished nothing in the face of the fast-deteriorating international situation. Nevertheless, before the final bankruptcy of disarmament as a means of securing world peace was revealed in the early 1930's, the United States was able to take the lead in organizing the most popular of all the steps in the movement against war.

In the Kellogg-Briand Pact the world's great powers, condemning recourse to war and renouncing it as an instrument of national policy, agreed that "the settlement of all disputes or conflicts . . . shall never be sought except by pacific means." This declaration signed at Paris on August 27, 1928, by 15 nations, and later by 48 others, was a striking example of the way in which the United States, despite its refusal to join the League of Nations, was willing nevertheless to cooperate with many of the League powers in such important matters as disarmament and the prevention of war. The United States Senate, it is true, made American membership in the World Court subject to reservations which prevented it from ever joining that tribunal, but the rising American support for increased international cooperation did achieve tangible results in the Kellogg-Briand Pact.

The origins of the Pact itself were really twofold. On the one hand, France sought a bilateral antiwar agreement with the United States as a means of improving its security in Europe. On the other hand, the Pact was at least a partial recognition of the long-standing pacifist demand that all war be declared a violation of international law. Just how the actual outlawry of war was to be enforced or made effective was unclear, but to an astonishing extent leading American scholars and diplomats hailed the Pact as a revolutionary breakthrough in international law. Some believed that it brought America closer to the League and the collective defense of the international status quo. Yet both England and France signed with the explicit understanding that the Pact left them free to defend their particular national security interests, and Secretary of State Kellogg on behalf of the United States admitted that "Every nation is free at all times and regardless of treaty provisions to defend its territory from attack or invasion and it alone is competent to decide whether circumstances require war in self-defense." [11]

As a symbol of the renunciation of war, it is by no means sure whether the Kellogg Pact was designed to arouse public support for peace and disarmament or merely to allay popular protests over the lagging progress in that direction. Later the Pact, so bitterly denounced as an example of pacifist wishful thinking, was used by Secretary Stimson in his protests against the Japanese march into Manchuria. Never wholly accepted in peace circles as a realistic measure since it froze the international status quo and did not provide for peaceful change, the Pact proved more useful as an instrument of American diplomatic and military policy than as a means of preserving world peace. Its final service came at the Nuremberg war-guilt trials when the Allied Tribunal after World War II was forced to use it as a basis of prosecution. All wars, preventive or defensive, just or unjust, were conveniently regarded as illegal only if they were waged after the Kellogg Pact. Thus the famous instrument for the renunciation of war found a belated and rather unintended utility. At the time of its signing, however, American opinion was clearly in favor of the Pact, and in the party platforms of 1928, Republicans stressed the contribution to peace made by President Coolidge and Secretary of State Frank B. Kellogg, while Democrats called for the "Outlawry of war and an abhorrence of militarism, conquest, and imperialism." [12]

Within America's own sphere of influence, and especially in the Caribbean area, the traditional military-diplomatic policy of the United States, like American foreign policy generally, could not resist the pacifism of the postwar era. In the face of increasingly strong protests at home which pointed to the contrast between the renunciation of war and militarist intervention in Latin America, the United States began to modify its former policies. Preparations were made to withdraw American troops from Nicaragua and Haiti, while long-standing differences with Mexico were negotiated. In 1930 the State Department published the significant *Memorandum on the Monroe Doctrine* completed in 1928 by J. Reuben Clark. This *Memorandum* in essence repudiated the Theodore Roosevelt

[11] Quoted in R. H. Ferrell, *Peace in Their Time* (New Haven, 1952), 174.

[12] *National Party Platforms, 1840–1960*, K. H. Porter and D. B. Johnson, eds. (Urbana, 1961), 273.

Corollary in which the Doctrine had been interpreted as giving the United States the right to intervene in Latin America. "The Doctrine," said Clark in describing the new view of Monroe's pronouncement, "states a case of the United States *vs.* Europe, and not the United States *vs.* Latin America." [13]

The changing United States attitude toward Latin America became more apparent in the 1930's. Under the Franklin D. Roosevelt Administration's philosophy of the Good Neighbor, the United States renounced intervention as a Latin American policy and moved to make the Monroe Doctrine the multilateral concern of all the American nations. Declining prospects for continued world peace and prosperity made Latin American trade and friendship of increasingly greater value and importance to the United States. At the same time, with fewer depression dollars available for foreign investment and with existing debts owed by Latin American nations in default, the old United States economic diplomacy undoubtedly became less attractive.

Despite such hopeful signs as the Good Neighbor policy in Latin America, the Kellogg Pact marked the close of an era in United States foreign affairs rather than the inauguration of a brave new world. After 1929 the deepening economic depression, the growing crisis in the Far East, the rise of Hitler in Germany, and the series of political changes within the governments of most of the world powers, all drastically altered the climate of international opinion in which the Pact was supposed to operate. The depression of the thirties upset the diplomacy of normalcy which had been based on the preservation of the economic status quo and on the maintenance of a delicate balance of power among the nation-states in Europe and Asia. So long as prosperity continued, militarism and navalism had been contained, but economic collapse invited the eventual resurgence of an aggressive, warlike diplomacy on the part of the dissatisfied world's powers.

Partial disarmament and the outlawry of war had been the most spectacular achievements of the postwar diplomacy, and in the 1920's both reflected the interests of American foreign policy and the mood of the American people. But in the 1930's the failure to

---

[13] J. R. Clark, *Memorandum on the Monroe Doctrine* (Washington, 1930), xxiv.

extend disarmament and the renewed threats of war in Asia and Europe brought about a shift in American thinking. Instead of cooperating to outlaw war in the world, Americans began to concentrate on the effort to keep the United States out of war. And American isolationism, more antiwar than ever, grew stronger as the American people reacted to the breakdown of the whole postwar system of international law and order.

During the four years of the Hoover Administration, the major test for American diplomacy in regard to the question of peace or war was undoubtedly the Manchurian affair. In 1929 a Russo-Chinese clash over the Chinese Eastern Railway in Manchuria had almost interfered with the promulgation of the Kellogg Pact. Two years later a more serious conflict between Japan and China led the Japanese army to take over the province of Manchuria, which Japan then subsequently recognized as the puppet state of Manchukuo. This armed intervention and conquest not only violated the Covenant of the League of Nations, but it also was contrary to the Kellogg Pact, which the Council of the League duly invoked in formally protesting the Japanese action. In support of the League Secretary of State Stimson notified Japan and China on January 7, 1932, that the United States could not "admit the legality" nor recognize any treaty respecting Manchuria which impaired its rights in China or which violated the Kellogg Pact. Stimson, who was determined to "put the situation morally in its right place," also drafted the famous open letter of February 23, 1932, to Senator Borah, in which he reviewed the principles of the American position in the Far East and urged support for the United States nonrecognition doctrine.[14]

In a strict sense nonrecognition was not a new policy, having already been applied, for example, against Mexico and Soviet Russia. By also invoking the Kellogg Pact, however, which had been endorsed by practically all countries, the United States under the Hoover-Stimson Doctrine was in a position to mobilize the moral

[14] *Peace and War: United States Foreign Policy, 1931–1941*, Department of State, ed. (Washington, 1943), 160, 168–173.

and legal force of world opinion against the Japanese aggression. Stimson, who was willing to go further in this regard than President Hoover, hoped to see some form of international economic sanctions or boycott applied against Japan. But England and France, though their stake in China was greater than that of the United States, were afraid to risk a conflict in the Far East, and President Hoover also objected strongly to economic coercion as the sure road to war.

Stimson's desire for a firmer policy against Japan, in contrast to the more cautious position taken by the League powers and President Hoover, brought into the open two differing conceptions of American foreign policy. American opinion, both official and unofficial, was still strongly against war, but there was now a major ideological split over the means by which this could best be achieved. Stimson's supporters believed that the United States should cooperate with the League of Nations in the effort to preserve international order and world peace. The United States, he declared in October, 1932, was "naturally destined for a leader in the promotion of peace throughout the world." In the instance of Manchuria, although he had certain misgivings, he was ready to have the United States support its moral and legal position by economic sanctions, and perhaps, if needed, by war. Ranged against Stimson's militant views were the powerful forces of American apathy and isolationism as well as the principled opposition of those who did not believe in fighting war with war. For most of the American people, the fate of Manchuria was of less concern than the possible war the United States might have to fight against Japan. Popular indifference toward events overseas was also encouraged in the midst of the depression by fears of the costs to American industry and agriculture of any economic boycott.

Despite the general pacifism which had made peace the highest ideal in American foreign policy since the First World War, and despite the knowledge that the United States would have to shoulder most of the burden in any collective action against Japan, there was nonetheless considerable support, especially in liberal internationalist and left-wing circles, for some kind of sanctions. Few saw, however, as William Neumann points out, that such a policy "carried the implications of another war in behalf of peace. Few saw that the Sino-Japanese relationship was too complex for a simple moral judgment by western nations with a stake in the Asian status quo, acquired by methods in the nineteenth century similar to those of Japan in the twentieth century." [15] The essential danger in Stimson's Far Eastern policy lay in the fact that it could not be carried out unless Japan was willing to back down and abandon what it considered its vital interests in China. Neither American opinion nor its military and economic forces were ready for a test of strength in the Pacific. Yet the United States, by assuming the lead in resisting Japan's advance, also incurred the major share of Japanese resentment and antagonism—feelings which grew steadily stronger until they exploded at Pearl Harbor. Meanwhile the non-recognition policy failed with respect to Manchuria, and it did not deter the Japanese from further aggression in China and the Far East.

By the close of the Hoover Administration and of Stimson's tenure as Secretary of State, the conflict in the Far East had become part of a general deterioration in the world settlement fashioned at the Paris Conference in 1919. The deepening economic depression of the thirties had the initial effect of diverting popular attention from foreign affairs and of discouraging diplomats from dealing imaginatively and resolutely with world problems. "More than any other single factor," Robert Ferrell writes, "the Great Depression explains the timidity of statesmanship in the crucial years from 1929 to 1933." [16] In the United States the Presidential election of 1932 took place with the country in the grip of the worst stages of its economic crisis. Accordingly, neither Hoover nor Roosevelt paid much attention to foreign affairs or indicated any major changes in American diplomacy.

Except for his continued adherence to the renunciation of war, President Roosevelt appeared to offer no consistent program with respect to foreign affairs in his first term of office. Domestic problems and economic considerations dictated diplomatic policy. A

[15] W. L. Neumann, *America Encounters Japan* (Baltimore, 1963), 197.
[16] Ferrell, *American Diplomacy in the Great Depression*, 5.

liberal program including such diverse steps as lower tariffs, the Good Neighbor policy, recognition of Soviet Russia, and Philippine independence was countered by nationalistic policies with respect to war debts, naval disarmament, and the London Economic Conference. At the Geneva Conference called by the League of Nations to consider at long last a general program of world-wide disarmament, American cooperation was not sufficient to stave off disaster. President Hoover's earlier offer of a comprehensive series of disarmament proposals failed to win support in the face of French demands for military security in Europe. Soon after his inauguration, however, President Roosevelt, in another effort to give life to the Conference, went so far as to suggest American help against aggressor nations if Europe disarmed. In a celebrated speech on May 22, 1933, Norman H. Davis, chairman of the United States delegation at Geneva, revealed this position. Indicating the possibility of America's becoming a part of the League's mechanism of collective security, Davis declared:

> In particular, we are willing to consult the other states in case of a threat to peace, with a view to averting conflict. Further than that, in the event that the states, in conference, determine that a state has been guilty of a breach of the peace in violation of its international obligations and take measures against the violator, then, if we concur in the judgment rendered as to the responsible and guilty party, we will refrain from any action tending to defeat such collective effort which these states may thus make to restore peace.[17]

Davis' offer, despite the brief flurry of excitement and hope that it provoked, bore no results and probably would not have had the backing of American public opinion or Congress. The United States Senate, for example, at this juncture refused to approve a discriminatory type of arms embargo to be applied against any or all belligerents in such a way, presumably, as to deter an aggressor nation from seeking to disturb the status quo. In any event, in the face of the Nazi movement in Germany and Hitler's assumption of power, the Conference was already on the way to becoming moribund. "After sixteen years the circle of frustration was closed. Efforts at world disarmament through the League had begun with the unilateral disarmament of Germany. The efforts ceased with the unilateral rearmament of Germany. The collective intelligence of Europe, having failed to achieve security, turned towards preparation for suicide." [18]

Unhappy over the rising militarism in Europe and Asia and over the failure of the Geneva Conference, the peace forces in the United States shifted their support from disarmament and the outlawry of war to the effort to isolate America from another World War—a conflict which many observers felt to be all but inevitable. Even convinced internationalists now lost confidence in the ability of the League of Nations to maintain the peace. At home the stock market crash and the ensuing Depression had deepened the growing popular distrust of American business values and methods and set the stage for the Nye Committee's investigation of the role of American bankers and munitions makers in the First World War. The widespread belief that selfish financial interests had led the country into war in 1917 strengthened demands for legislation to take the profits out of war. The Neutrality Acts of the late 1930's were an important result of this heritage of American disillusionment over World War I. Reflecting the turn toward an isolationist peace, they rested on the determination of the country to try to prevent propaganda and economic interests from again influencing American diplomacy.

Almost since the close of the First World War, Congress had given some attention to various means of avoiding United States participation in another great international struggle. Most popular were plans to control the munitions industry and all wartime profits and to place an embargo on the export of arms to belligerents. But the first of the formal Neutrality Acts was not approved until August, 1935. This law was a temporary emergency measure passed largely in response to fears that American neutrality would be jeopardized as a result of the Italo-Ethiopian crisis. It provided that whenever the President should proclaim the existence of a state of war the sale or transportation of arms and munitions to the belligerents should be prohibited. Travel on belligerent ships by United States citizens might also be subjected to government restriction.

In February, 1936, Congress widened the original Neutrality Act by also prohibiting loans to belligerents. And on January 8,

[18] F. L. Schuman, *International Politics*, 3rd ed. (New York, 1941), 479.

1937, it hastily approved a joint resolution forbidding the export of munitions "for the use of either of the opposing forces" in the Spanish Civil War. Then in spring of 1937 Congress passed a so-called permanent neutrality act with little opposition. This measure retained the prohibitions on munitions, loans, and travel, but it added the provision that for a period of two years such raw materials as the President might list could be taken from the United States by the belligerents on a "cash and carry" basis. Most significantly, however, the 1937 Act continued to withhold from the President the discriminatory feature which would have permitted him to apply an arms embargo in a selective fashion, thereby invoking it against one or another set of belligerents.

In a strict sense the Neutrality Acts, especially with the added cash and carry feature, were a compromise with true neutrality. In the words of Senator Borah, "We seek to avoid all risks, all dangers, but we make certain to get all the profits." "What sort of government is this," asked Hiram Johnson, "and what sort of men are we to accept a formula which will enable us to sell goods and then hide? . . . We take the profits and then hug ourselves because somebody else has to take the risk." [19] The Neutrality Acts, more antiwar than neutral, reflected the American desire to enjoy the profits and relative safety of peace without its costs or risks. Potentially unneutral, even without the discriminatory clause desired by President Roosevelt, the measures with their cash and carry provision came close to violating the whole premise on which the legislation was originally based. Yet the Neutrality Acts, though watered down and subject to a wide variety of criticism, had the strong support of Congress and the country. Although few discerning observers believed that the Acts were a guarantee against American involvement in another world conflict, they did provide certain safeguards against the kind of incidents that had led to American participation in the First World War.

From the standpoint of traditional American foreign policy, the Neutrality Acts were revolutionary and controversial measures, yielding almost without qualification the nation's historic insistence on its right as a neutral to carry on a normal trade in wartime. Even Jefferson's celebrated embargo had been an effort to secure these

---

[19] March 1, 3, 1937, *Congressional Record*, 75 Cong., 1 Sess., 1677, 1778.

rights by temporary self-restrictions on American trade. By 1935, however, America's willingness to surrender its dictum of "free ships make free goods" was in large part a result of Woodrow Wilson's discriminatory and unneutral methods of trying to enforce American rights in World War I. The legislation of the 1930's accordingly was a belated effort by the American people, born of their disillusionment with the First World War, to avoid a repetition of that unhappy experience. This expectation might have been realized if, in fact, the neutrality legislation of the thirties had remained true to the ideas of most of its early supporters. A measure enforcing a complete and rigid embargo equally upon all belligerents, and including raw materials as well as munitions without the modification of cash and carry provisions, conceivably could have kept the United States neutral. But the American people could hardly have been expected to endure the economic sacrifices which such an ascetic, astringent foreign policy would have exacted. Thus the most important fallacy concerning the Neutrality Acts was the popular notion that they automatically were able to enforce a strict and impartial neutrality.

While President Roosevelt signed the various neutrality bills, there is abundant evidence that he was unhappy over Congressional insistence upon a relatively inflexible type of arms embargo which had to be applied equally to all belligerents. He shared the view of the State Department that any neutrality legislation should be selective, permitting the President to apply an embargo against the belligerents in such a discriminatory fashion that only those nations which the United States deemed nonaggressors would receive arms. Such a provision, which was refused repeatedly by Congress until 1939 when munitions as well as raw materials were put on a cash and carry basis, of course made a mockery of true neutrality. Although a selective embargo of the sort desired by the President and the State Department had nothing to do with neutrality, it is important to note, however, that it did not contest what was the central idea behind all the legislation—the renunciation of war.

Essentially hostile to the idea of continued American isolation, the President nevertheless hoped to be able to keep the United States out of war. Behind the kind of discriminatory embargo which he desired was the State Department's belief that the so-called aggressor nations could be deterred from going to war by the knowledge that American arms and munitions would be sent only to those countries committed to the preservation of the peace and status quo in Europe and Asia. In practice, the great potential military power of the United States would be made available to resist the expansionist designs of Japan in the Far East and of Germany on the continent of Europe. The President wanted to keep the United States at peace by preventing war from breaking out in the rest of the world. Congress on the other hand, without committing itself to such an effort, desired to use the neutrality laws to keep the United States out of any and all foreign wars.

Although Congress refused Roosevelt's request to repeal the mandatory arms embargo until after war had actually begun in Europe in September, 1939, the President was usually able to interpret the legislation to suit the desired ends of his own foreign policies. In the Italian war against Ethiopia, the first Neutrality Act with its embargo on arms, but not on raw materials, proved futile. The moral pressure exerted by the State Department to halt shipments of oil and other strategic goods to Italy was likewise ineffective. Even more, the United States' attempt to cooperate with the League of Nations program of economic sanctions had the effect chiefly of antagonizing Italy and of uniting its people behind what had been an unpopular war. At the same time, in going beyond the restrictions of its own law, the United States acted in what was an unneutral manner in its vain effort to hamper Italy and to try to aid Ethiopia. In the case of the Spanish Civil War, the application of the embargo to both sides departed from American past practice, as evidenced in Latin America by refusing arms only to the revolutionary or insurgent faction in a domestic dispute. Despite its pretense of impartiality, American policy regarding the Spanish Civil War was in reality an unneutral discrimination against the legal Loyalist Government. Finally, with respect to the renewal of the Japanese attack on China, the United States, by taking advantage of the fact that Japan had not formally declared war, was able to continue to send munitions to China. Here American policy again was unneutral since the effect of the President's not invoking the law was to provide at least some aid to China.

In every major conflict which broke out while the Neutrality Acts were in force, it may be said that United States policy was in fact unneutral—a situation which the laws themselves, as they were written, could hardly have prevented. Ineffective in regard to the Italo-Ethiopian war, unfair as applied to the Civil War in Spain, and not invoked in the Sino-Japanese conflict, the Neutrality Acts reflected only the illusion of American neutrality. Whatever the popular expectations regarding foreign policy, American diplomacy in the thirties was moving steadily away from the practice of an impartial neutrality.

Although the logical end of President Roosevelt's unneutral diplomacy suggested American belligerency if another World War broke out, the President in his speeches in 1935 and 1936 continued to give support to disarmament and to reject war as an instrument of American foreign policy. By the mid-1930's antiwar feeling in the United States was at its peak. Public opinion polls showed an overwhelming sentiment against American entrance into any foreign war as well as the continued belief that participation in the First World War had been a mistake. In the spring of 1936 Senator Key Pittman, chairman of the Senate Foreign Relations Committee, declared bluntly: "Our government will not send its military forces to Europe in aid of the enforcement of the decrees of the League of Nations or any other league or alliance, even though that be the only way to punish a guilty aggressor and prevent or stop war." [20] And the Democrats in their party platform adopted a strong peace plank in which it was asserted:

We shall continue to observe a true neutrality in the disputes of others; to be prepared resolutely to resist aggression against ourselves; to work for peace and to take the profits out of war; to guard against being drawn, by political commitments, international banking, or private trading, into any war which may develop anywhere.[21]

The President himself, in his campaign for reelection, though giving little time to foreign policy, stressed his basic renunciation

[20] Quoted in R. N. Stromberg, *Collective Security and American Foreign Policy* (New York, 1963), 108.
[21] *National Party Platforms*, 363.

of war. At Chautauqua on August 14, 1936, he reviewed at length the efforts of his administration to cooperate in the search for world peace. The United States, he pointed out, continued to "shun political commitments which might entangle us in foreign wars. . . . We are not isolationists," the President added,

except insofar as we seek to isolate ourselves completely from war. Yet we must remember that so long as war exists on earth there will be some danger that even the nation which most ardently desires peace may be drawn into war.

I have seen war. I have seen war on land and sea. I have seen blood running from the wounded. I have seen men coughing out their gassed lungs. I have seen the dead in the mud. I have seen cities destroyed. I have seen 200 limping, exhausted men come out of line—the survivors of a regiment of 1,000 that went forward 48 hours before. I have seen children starving. I have seen the agony of mothers and wives. I hate war.[22]

Although in the excitement of campaigning Roosevelt exaggerated his own intimate contact with the effects of war, there is no reason to doubt his strong personal revulsion of its horrors. He reminded his listeners that, despite the Neutrality Acts, "the effective maintenance of American neutrality depends today, as in the past, on the wisdom and determination of whoever at the moment occupy the offices of President and Secretary of State. . . . We can keep out of war," Roosevelt concluded, "if those who watch and decide have a sufficiently detailed understanding of international affairs to make certain that the small decisions of each day do not lead toward war, and if, at the same time, they possess the courage to say 'no' to those who selfishly or unwisely would let us go to war." [23]

At New York City the President, in closing his campaign for reelection, spoke out with even greater force against war. After summarizing again the domestic accomplishments of his administration, he declared:

All this—all these objectives—spell peace at home. All our actions, all our ideals, spell also peace with other nations.

Today there is war and rumor of war. We want none of it. . . . You know well that those who stand to profit by war are not on our side in this campaign.

22 *Peace and War*, 325–326.
23 *Ibid.*, 325–329.

'Peace on earth, good will toward men'—democracy must cling to that message. . . .

That is the road to peace.[24]

Despite this final note of renunciation, however, it was plain that the President felt the issue of war in United States foreign policy might be affected more by the international situation than by America's own devotion to peace and neutrality. Essentially peace depended, as he said, on the wisdom and will of the Chief Executive and here Roosevelt, it became increasingly clear after 1936, believed that America must take up the cause of a new, more militant world leadership as well as continuing to renounce war. This dual role for American diplomacy was part of the same curious paradox, described by Carl Becker as "Loving Peace and Waging War," [25] which had faced the American people in the years before 1917. On the horns of this dilemma, American foreign policy entered upon the troubled period of the Second World War.

SELECTED REFERENCES

Adler, Selig. *The Isolationist Impulse: Its Twentieth-Century Reaction.* New York: Abelard-Schuman, 1957.

Beard, Charles A. *American Foreign Policy in the Making, 1932–1940: A Study in Responsibilities.* New Haven: Yale University Press, 1946.

Borchard, Edwin and W. P. Lage. *Neutrality for the United States.* New Haven: Yale University Press, 1940.

Current, Richard N. *Secretary Stimson: A Study in Statecraft.* New Brunswick, N.J.: Rutgers University Press, 1954.

DeConde, Alexander, ed. *Isolation and Security: Ideas and Interests in Twentieth-Century American Foreign Policy.* Durham, N.C.: Duke University Press, 1957.

Divine, Robert A. *The Illusion of Neutrality.* Chicago: University of Chicago Press, 1962.

Ferrell, Robert H. *American Diplomacy in the Great Depression: Hoover-Stimson Foreign Policy, 1929–1933.* New Haven: Yale University Press, 1957.

[24] *Public Papers and Addresses of Franklin D. Roosevelt,* S. I. Rosenman, ed. (New York, 1938–1950), V, 572–573.

[25] *Yale Review,* XXVI (June, 1937), 649–668.

————. *Peace in Their Time: The Origins of the Kellogg-Briand Pact.* New Haven: Yale University Press, 1952.

Sprout, Harold and Margaret. *Toward a New Order of Sea Power: American Naval Policy and the World Scene, 1918–1922.* Princeton: Princeton University Press, 1940.

Tate, Merze. *The United States and Armaments.* Cambridge, Mass.: Harvard University Press, 1948.

Vinson, John C. *The Parchment Peace: The United States Senate and the Washington Conference, 1921–1922.* Athens: University of Georgia Press, 1955.

————. *William E. Borah and the Outlawry of War.* Athens: University of Georgia Press, 1957.

Wheeler, Gerald E. *Prelude to Pearl Harbor: The United States Navy and the Far East.* Columbia, Missouri: University of Missouri Press, 1963.

Wiltz, John E. *In Search of Peace: The Senate Munitions Inquiry, 1934–36.* Baton Rouge: Louisiana State University Press, 1963.

VIII

World Leadership
Under Arms

The general American renunciation of war in the twenties and thirties was succeeded by a new era in which war, or the threat of war, again dominated the world. To an extent unparalleled in their history, the American people learned to live in the midst of international strife and conflict. The United States assumed a new position of world leadership in large part through military strength, while the American mission itself was placed under arms. In regard to such historic postulates of United States foreign policy as nonintervention, disarmament, and neutrality, Americans reversed their older, post-World War I beliefs and opinions. And, despite their bitter disillusionment over the First World War, they gave their support, reluctantly at first and then with growing enthusiasm, to what was an increasingly interventionist foreign policy. Well before the attack on Pearl Harbor, President Roosevelt already was urging world leadership upon the United States, and such leadership, greatly strengthened during the Second World War, remained the most important consideration in American postwar diplomacy. Henry Luce's vision of an "American Century," long the dream of certain publicists and patriots, seemed suddenly a more real possibility than at any time in the past as a major share of the earth's surface came under the influence of American ideas and interests.

The amazing transformation in popular thinking in regard to the role of the United States on questions of peace or war was in general a response to the changing world situation. In the face of new developments threatening the status quo in Europe and Asia by the late 1930's, the United States, despite its continued renunciation of war as an instrument of foreign policy, steadily became less neutral, less isolationist, and less pacific. The major diplomatic problem for the United States and the other democracies of the West—mainly England and France—was to prevent the rise to dominance of the dictator nations—the defeated Germany and Russia, and the dissatisfied victors, Italy and Japan. Fortunately for the Western democracies, the totalitarian powers were divided during most of the thirties by the ideological conflicts of fascism versus communism, and by their own natural rivalries over China and Eastern Europe. At the same time, however, though the West was united in its desire to preserve the Versailles settlement, it was not able to agree on the necessary practical steps to that end. Accordingly most of the suggested policies looking toward collective defense and mutual security against the dictatorships were far from realistic. Even collective security, although it won increasing acceptance in the United States as a part of a program of American world leadership, was no automatic solution for the world's ills.

Like isolationism in American foreign policy, collective security was not without its fallacies and myths. First and foremost, according to an extended recent analysis by Roland Stromberg, a policy of collective security under American leadership had to be justified as a means of preventing war. Unless one took the absurd position that it was justifiable to prevent one war by waging another, one had to claim that a show of force sometime in the 1930's would have deterred the aggressors and thus avoided eventual hostilities. Mere words or an inadequate appeasement, however, would hardly have impressed Japan, Italy, or Germany in the late 1930's, and whether the Second World War could have been fought earlier and on terms more favorable to the West is at least doubtful. Secondly, even the so-called fact of Nazi aggression was not always clear and was clouded by claims of German self-determination and World War I injustice. Thirdly, in any collective police action the disinterest of the policeman is assumed, but a powerful handicap to League action against Germany as well as Japan was the fear that Soviet Russia would be the nation to reap the most benefit. Collective security against the aggressors was hardly feasible without Soviet help, yet the results of such help seemed certain to result in the very Russian expansion of which the West later complained after World War II. Finally, the assumption that a stand against Japan in Manchuria or against Italy in Ethiopia would have deterred other aggressors, chiefly Nazi Germany, is by no means necessarily valid. For example, American action against Japan might well have encouraged Germany to move more swiftly in Europe while the United States was tied down in the Far East. It is also arguable that the limited degree of united action taken against Italy in 1935 under the League of Nations was responsible for driving her into the Axis camp.

In the case of Nazi Germany, firmness on the part of the West at the time of Hitler's reoccupation of the Rhineland in 1936 might have yielded better results than firmness at the time of Munich. As George Kennan has pointed out, however, it is possible "to exaggerate the relative importance of this question of stopping Hitler once he was in power, as compared with the importance of seeing to it that a person of his ilk should not come into power at all in a great Western country." [1] The great misfortune of the West was that it did not revise its foreign policies, particularly the Treaty of Versailles, and strengthen the German Republic before its weaknesses paved the way for Hitler's assumption of power. In the era between wars, collective security, according to E. H. Carr writing in 1939, was a device for confusing the real issues and concealing the "vested interests" of the satisfied powers.

In the past, Roman and British imperialism were commended to the world in the guise of the *pax Romana* and the *pax Britannica*. To-day, when no single Power is strong enough to dominate the world, and supremacy is vested in a group of nations, slogans like "collective security" and "resistance to aggression" serve the same purpose of proclaiming an identity of interest between the dominant group and the world as a whole in the maintenance of peace.[2]

Despite its limitations in the 1930's, collective security was later endowed with many of the qualities of an absolute truth in the opinion of a number of students of American diplomacy. At the same time, enthusiastic proponents of a policy of American world leader-

[1] G. F. Kennan, *American Diplomacy, 1900–1950* (Chicago, 1951), 79.
[2] E. H. Carr, *The Twenty Years' Crisis, 1919–1939* (London, 1939), 104.

ship alleged that the pacifist and isolationist forces in the United States in the thirties, in their opposition to collective security, had helped to bring on World War II. These groups, it was asserted, in the depths of their disillusionment over the First World War, had undermined American patriotism and popular willingness to fight and support American leadership in the Second Great Crusade. Pacifists and isolationists, it was true, had sometimes been unrealistic in their belief or hope that the renunciation of war would be able to prevail over selfish national interests. But few were so idealistic or naïve that they failed to understand the relation of power and economic interests to modern war. Despairing of any easy solution and convinced after the mid-1930's that the qualified and limited degree of collective security practiced by the West could not safeguard the peace, the isolationist and pacifist forces urged neutrality as, on the whole, the soundest and safest policy for the United States. Thus they refused to accept the idea of American world leadership as the best means of preventing war at home or abroad.

Although the search for peace and security in the midst of the unfavorable international climate was the major factor influencing the diplomacy of the United States, foreign affairs in the 1930's were also affected by conditions within each country's own political economy. Especially during the years of the Depression, no nation could conduct its foreign policy without attention to the various stresses and strains to which diplomacy might be subjected on the home front. In the United States the Roosevelt Administration's economic recovery program was related to foreign as well as domestic concerns. And, as the New Deal seemed to reach its ideological limits after Roosevelt's first term, Mars came to the rescue, transforming earlier visions of peaceful reform into a war economy. According to the interesting time chart which historian Dexter Perkins worked out to illustrate "a cyclical theory of American foreign policy," the years after 1937, in contrast to the pacific feeling of the previous decade, were ones characterized by rising bellicosity, war, and postwar nationalism. Professor Perkins also noted that wars seemed to come after depressions and in periods of a post-depression economic upswing, with the greatest risk to peace apparently in the recovery periods.[3]

For example, by the late 1930's, the United States and other Western nations were climbing out of the depths of the Depression. In the first shock of the economic crisis in 1929 and 1930, governments had concentrated upon their domestic problems, while peoples almost everywhere looked upon armaments as an unnecessary extravagance. The Depression initially destroyed much of the will of the West for war. It encouraged the kind of conciliatory foreign policy and economizing illustrated in the Hoover Administration's attempts at disarmament. But the long-range effect of the world's economic collapse in the 1930's nevertheless pointed toward war. Ultimately the Depression stimulated the forces of nationalism, encouraged rearmament, and accentuated the rival antagonisms and ambitions of the great powers. Popular discontents, politicians and statesmen perceived, could be relieved in some measure by the diversion of public attention to foreign affairs. Militarism and navalism were more susceptible of widespread approval if the ensuing rearmament programs could be explained in terms not only of achieving preparedness, but also of relieving unemployment and fostering economic recovery.

In varying degrees in the 1930's countries nationalized their economies through increasing governmental regulation and centralized planning. And, the planned economy was easily adapted to war. As Walter Lippmann pointed out in 1937 in his book *The Good Society*, "though the planned economy is proposed as a form of social organization which will provide peace and plenty, thus far in all its concrete manifestations it has been associated with scarcity and war. From 1914 to 1918 all the belligerents were driven step by step into a planned and politically directed economy. . . ." Now again, he noted, even in those "nations which are still democratic and capitalistic, plans are drawn for their rapid transformation into totalitarian states." [4]

In the United States industrial mobilization, originally conceived as a plan to take the profits out of war and thus to try to

[3] Dexter Perkins, *The American Approach to Foreign Policy* (Cambridge, Mass., 1952), Chap. 7.

[4] Walter Lippmann, *An Inquiry into the Principles of the Good Society* (Boston, 1937), 89.

prevent it, became an avenue of economic preparedness for war. Naval experts advised the diplomats at the disarmament conferences, and in general the popular desire for peace had little effect in circumscribing military policy. Under the New Deal the military and naval budget was expanded indirectly by the use of funds appropriated for the N.R.A., P.W.A., and W.P.A. In the case of the relief program directed by Harry Hopkins, his biographer has written that "despite the prohibitions against any military activities which had been written into the Work Relief Bill, W.P.A. accomplished a great deal of construction—airports, highways, bridges, etc.—that had deliberately strategic importance." [5] Encouragement for American world leadership and a more aggressive foreign policy was also provided by a program of naval building as well as in the greater activity in detailed planning for war on a global scale carried on by the Army General Staff, the Navy Board, and the War Colleges.

To the general American public, still isolationist in temper and absorbed in such domestic affairs as the New Deal's struggle with the Supreme Court, the first major portent pointing to United States world leadership was President Roosevelt's so-called Quarantine Speech at Chicago on October 5, 1937. In this major address on foreign policy, the President, in effect, "broke with isolationism, discarded the policy of strict neutrality, and stepped forward as an advocate of collective security." [6] Despite continued strong public backing for peace and neutrality, the Roosevelt Administration had gradually been moving toward a more positive formulation of American foreign policy. The isolationism implied in the neutrality legislation had received at best only qualified support from the Administration, except in the rhetoric of the President's 1936 campaign speeches. And, as Secretary of State Hull explained soon after the passage of the first Neutrality Act, the United States could not be unconcerned over such events as the Italo-Ethiopian War. America, he declared,

[5] Robert Sherwood, *Roosevelt and Hopkins* (New York, 1948), 75.

[6] W. L. Langer and S. E. Gleason, *The Challenge to Isolation* (New York, 1952), 18.

should not concentrate entirely on means for remaining neutral and lose sight of other constructive methods of avoiding involvement in wars between other countries. Our foreign policy would indeed be a weak one if it began or ended with the announcement of a neutral position on the outbreak of a foreign war. I conceive it to be our duty and in the interest of our country and of humanity, not only to remain aloof from disputes and conflicts with which we have no direct concern, but also to use our influence in any appropriate way to bring about the peaceful settlement of international differences. Our own interest and our duty as a great power forbid that we shall sit idly by and watch the development of hostilities with a feeling of self-sufficiency and complacency when by the use of our influence, short of becoming involved in the dispute itself, we might prevent or lessen the scourge of war.[7]

By the fall of 1937 it was increasingly obvious that the world order fashioned by the Versailles Treaty and at the Washington Conference was breaking down. Rearmament rather than disarmament had become the new international reality, and in Europe and Asia alike it was clear that Germany and Japan would no longer consider themselves bound by the efforts of the League of Nations to enforce the status quo. Instead, they joined with Italy in 1936 in an anti-Comintern pact directed at Soviet Russia, and in the summer of 1937 Japan resumed large-scale military operations in China. In the United States President Roosevelt, like Secretary Hull, did not accept the popular isolationist view that a neutral America could automatically stay out of any future world conflict. Until his address at Chicago, however, he refrained from calling upon the United States to play a major role in leading the world to a "triumph of law and moral principles in order that peace, justice, and confidence may prevail. . . ."

Despite its secure position, "the people of the United States under modern conditions must, for the sake of their own future, give thought to the rest of the world. . . ." In the President's words:

The peace-loving nations must make a concerted effort in opposition to those violations of treaties and those ignorings of humane instincts which today are creating a state of international anarchy and instability from which there is no escape through mere isolation or neutrality. . . .

The situation is definitely of universal concern. . . .

[7] *Peace and War: United States Foreign Policy, 1931–1941*, Department of State, ed. (Washington, 1943), 286.

It seems to be unfortunately true that the epidemic of world lawlessness is spreading.

When an epidemic of physical disease starts to spread, the community
approves and joins in a quarantine of the patients in order to protect the
health of the community against the spread of the disease.

It is my determination to pursue a policy of peace and to adopt every
practicable measure to avoid involvement in war. . . .

America hates war. America hopes for peace. Therefore, America actively engages in the search for peace.[8]

What Roosevelt meant by the term "quarantine" or what he
hoped to accomplish in his speech was not clear. At the very least it
was perhaps merely a trial balloon, launched to help gauge the
winds of public sentiment. More probably the President hoped to
win popular support for a firm United States policy in dealing with
Japan and in deterring Hitler in Europe. At the most the speech
portended the use of economic sanctions and even war against the
Japanese. Later, in 1939, the United States did abrogate its commercial treaty with Japan and place an unofficial moral embargo
on most war materials. In the meantime American consumers
responded with a private economic boycott on Japanese goods. Thus,
well before Pearl Harbor, the United States was already engaged in
full-scale economic warfare against Japan.

In the fall of 1937, however, popular reaction to Roosevelt's
sensational speech remained uncertain and confused. Advocates of
vigorous action against Japan applauded the President's view that
"There must be positive endeavors to preserve peace," while isolationists denounced the speech as warmongering inconsistent with the
Neutrality Acts. As a result of the speech, the peace movement was
split more than ever between its isolationist and internationalist
wings. On all sides, moreover, there was the growing fear that unless
a collective security program was intended only as a colossal bluff
or meaningless verbal threat, it would require the United States to
build up its armed forces for possible use against those powers
deemed aggressor nations. Meanwhile the generally favorable newspaper comment across the country was qualified by the fact that
most of the editorial writers were in doubt as to what the President's
speech really implied. Roosevelt and the State Department, in turn,
were disappointed over the failure of the speech to arouse greater

8 *Ibid.*, 383–387.

public enthusiasm and unity for the Administration's foreign policy.

From a practical diplomatic point of view, the new American foreign policy suggested in the Quarantine Speech achieved only meager accomplishments. At Brussels in November, 1937, an international conference of the major Far Eastern powers was unwilling to do more than condemn Japan's latest invasion of China. At the same time President Roosevelt's ambitious plans for calling a worldwide disarmament and peace conference also had to be abandoned in the face of unfavorable prospects for its success. Although the Roosevelt Administration made clear its support of Great Britain and France, there was no realistic possibility of American action in Europe to resist German demands. Taking advantage of the widespread uncertainty among his opponents as to what their most desirable course of action should be—whether appeasement in the West or a united front with Russia in the East—Hitler was able to move steadily forward toward securing German goals on the Continent, while Japan plunged ahead in China. America's initial efforts to invoke moral pressure without any stronger commitment to further action probably only antagonized Japan and the Axis powers. The United States, it seemed, was willing to talk peace but not to assume the burdens of leadership. Thus it was "in the position of pushing policies that might well lead to war, while abjuring all responsibility for such a war." [9]

The continued strong popular support for neutrality stood against the President's desire to see the United States participate in some form of collective world action against Japan and Germany. Even the Japanese bombing of the American gunboat *Panay* on December 12, 1937, provoked what was, on the whole, a mild public reaction, especially in contrast to the popular furor over such incidents in past American history. That antiwar sentiment was also still the dominant feeling in Congress was illustrated in the growing enthusiasm for passage of the Ludlow Amendment. This amendment proposed to revise the Constitution by providing a nationwide referendum before the United States could declare war. Long a popular cause in peace circles, Ludlow's proposal was finally brought to a vote in the House of Representatives on January 10, 1938.

[9] R. N. Stromberg, *Collective Security and American Foreign Policy* (New York, 1963), 120.

Then on a motion to release the bill from committee, it was defeated, 209 to 188, but only after the White House exerted the strongest possible political pressures upon individual Congressmen.

The dilemmas of American foreign policy in the midst of the quickening tempo of the world crisis were matched by increasing economic and political frustrations at home. In 1937 another severe economic slump was overcome only by the resumption of heavy Government spending. Amid signs that popular support for many of the New Deal's relief and public works projects was waning, defense appropriations became more important to the health of the American domestic economy. The Roosevelt Administration, it seemed, was becoming ever more willing to let war orders take care of the depression.

Despite his overwhelming victory in the 1936 elections, the President's prestige was weakened by a series of subsequent political defeats. For example, the bitter fight over the plan to revamp the Supreme Court split the Democratic party and helped create a conservative bloc in Congress which was able to defeat most further domestic reform legislation. Then the President's attempts to strengthen the New Deal by his personal campaign against conservative Democrats in the 1938 party primaries backfired disastrously. In the mid-term elections the Republicans gained 81 seats in the House and eight in the Senate. At a time of international crisis in 1938 and 1939, symbolized in the false hopes of Munich, Roosevelt therefore appeared to be losing the support of broad sections of the American electorate. As some of his political magic seemingly declined, however, the President was able to turn to a new phase of his career. "Quietly abandoning his New Deal reforms, which had become the primary source of internal dissension, he set out to unite both conservatives and liberals behind a program of national preparedness designed to meet the dangers facing the United States in the international arena." [10]

Shortly after the defeat of the Ludlow War Referendum, Presi-

[10] R. A. Divine, *The Illusion of Neutrality* (Chicago, 1962), 230–231.

dent Roosevelt on January 28, 1938, asked Congress for new naval legislation to back up his foreign policy. In a special message he called for further increases in naval armaments and for legislation aimed at "the prevention of profiteering in time of war and the equalization of the burdens of possible war." [11] In fact, as the isolationists in Congress well understood, the President proposed to carry out a vigorous American foreign policy, asserting the kind of world leadership he had already suggested in his Quarantine Speech. For practical political reasons, however, the idea of collective security was subordinated to the concept of national defense. The Administration realized that it would be easier to overcome the still strong isolationist feelings of the public if American world leadership was explained primarily in terms of national security at home.

Although the threat of war was imminent only in Europe and Asia, popular support for a policy of combining programs of collective security and national defense came most readily in connection with Latin America. Under the diplomacy of the Good Neighbor, United States trade treaties had replaced military intervention as a means of strengthening hemispheric ties, and at the several Inter-American Conferences in the 1930's plans were worked out for the mutual defense of the American republics. On December 24, 1938, the twenty-one republics accordingly approved the Declaration of Lima, reaffirming their determination to defend themselves "against all foreign intervention or activity that may threaten them," and proclaiming their common concern "in case the peace, security or territorial integrity of any American republic" was menaced.[12]

A broad program committing the United States to the defense of the Western Hemisphere was a useful means of countering popular suspicions of foreign policies which went beyond the defense of the continental United States. In the words of an official Army historian: "It was wiser to ask Congress for support in defending the South American approach to the Canal than in providing resistance to Hitler elsewhere: it was more visibly a 'defensive' measure." Hemispheric defense also "helped materially to provide an

[11] *Peace and War*, 404.
[12] *Ibid.*, 440.

escape from the old idea of 'national' defense and a basic change in concept from passive defense to a dynamic defense designed to go into action before the enemy could launch his attack, and this was a vital change." [13]

In the area of the forty-eight states and its North American possessions, the United States was hardly unprepared. The Navy had been rebuilding since 1934, and by the end of the decade the United States outstripped Japan by a considerable margin in battleships and submarines. During most of the 1930's the Navy had received all or more than it requested of Congress in the way of appropriations, and the outbreak of war in Europe found the United States well on the way to having a two-ocean fleet. In April, 1941, a Foreign Policy Report asserted: "The scope of the Navy's plans for expansion can scarcely be depicted without use of superlatives." [14] By this time the Army had a trained nucleus of regulars and reserves with plans for its increase via Selective Service, while the Air Force, despite a seeming unreadiness because of rapid expansion and the diversion of production to England, was qualified for combat and fully capable of protecting the United States. As the isolationists in Congress pointed out in the course of the long debate over the naval rearmament program in 1938, American military preparedness was being carried beyond the purely defensive needs of the country. In actual fact, it was tied to the diplomacy of collective security and to the ambitious plans for American world leadership in wartime as well as in peace.

Despite his stress on the military security of the United States within the framework of the Western Hemisphere, President Roosevelt continued to attack the concepts of isolationism and absolute neutrality. In his opening address to Congress on January 4, 1939, he warned that national defense alone was not enough to stem aggression:

Words may be futile, but war is not the only means of commanding a decent respect for the opinions of mankind. There are many methods short of war, but stronger and more effective than mere words, of bringing home to aggressor governments the aggregate sentiments of our own people.

[13] M. S. Watson, *The War Department Chief of Staff: Prewar Plans and Preparations* (Washington, 1950), 95–96.

[14] D. H. Popper, "America's Naval Preparedness," *Foreign Policy Reports*, XVII (April 1, 1941), 14.

At the very least, we can and should avoid any action, or any lack of action, which will encourage, assist, or build up an aggressor.[15]

Revision of the Neutrality Laws to permit England and France to secure American munitions in the event of war was obviously what the President had in mind. But the strong outcry against his suggestion of "methods short of war" and the continued isolationism in Congress resulted finally, after months of debate, in the temporary defeat of the Administration's efforts to secure repeal of the mandatory arms embargo.

Congress' negative vote on the repeal measure in June, 1939, preceded by only a few months the long-expected outbreak of open conflict in Europe. After Hitler marched his legions into Poland, expansion of America's own military might was of less immediate importance to United States foreign policy than the question of whether Congress would reverse its action and modify the Neutrality Laws to help the "victims of aggression" and hamper the "aggressors." Although President Roosevelt issued the proclamation of formal neutrality required by international law and the United States Neutrality Act of 1937, in a radio address to the country he stated that he could not "ask that every American remain neutral in thought as well." Roosevelt's acceptance of a frank unneutrality contrasted with Wilson's 1914 admonition to the American people to be "impartial in thought as well as in action." Motivated by sympathy for the Allies, the President called Congress into special session to revise the Neutrality Act and repeal the embargo on the export of munitions. At the same time, he gave his personal assurance "that by the repeal of the embargo the United States will more probably remain at peace than if the law remains as it stands today."[16]

Once hostilities in Europe had become a fact, the United States, as the favorable vote on the repeal of the embargo indicated, was in the curious position of desiring the defeat of Hitler without

[15] *Peace and War,* 449.
[16] *Ibid.,* 485, 487.

actually going to war. "What a majority of the American people want," wrote Freda Kirchwey in the *Nation*, "is to be as unneutral as possible without getting into war." [17] William Allen White's Committee to Defend America by Aiding the Allies eventually became an interventionist organization looking to full-scale American participation in the War. But at the outset White, the chairman of the group, thought of aid to the Western democracies as a means of defeating Hitler without bringing the United States into the War. In the face of the German victories in the spring of 1940 and the fall of France, however, this limited interventionist position became difficult to maintain.

In the Presidential campaign of 1940 Roosevelt and Wendell Willkie, the Republican candidate, outdid each other in making lavish promises that American boys would not be sent to fight across the oceans. But the passage of the Selective Service Act in September, together with a military and naval budget unprecedented for its size, was a better indication of the direction and scope of American foreign policy. Even more significant in this regard was the Destroyer-for-Bases-Agreement providing for the immediate transfer of fifty destroyers to Great Britain in return for ninety-nine year leases on air and naval stations in British Newfoundland and on British islands in the Caribbean. The destroyer-base deal violated both the traditional United States neutrality which Wilson had championed in 1914 and the neutrality legislation enacted by Congress after 1935. The transfer was so unneutral, Winston Churchill later conceded in 1949, that "according to all the standards of history," Germany would have been justified in declaring war against the United States.[18] In explaining his course of action, however, in which he was motivated by the increasingly desperate plight of England, President Roosevelt stressed the importance of the new bases to the security of the United States.

The concept of defense was indeed being pushed to its outermost limits as the United States sought every possible means to provide greater material aid to Britain. Less fearful of isolationist criticisms once the elections were safely over, Roosevelt prepared to take another of his historic steps short of war. In a "Fireside

---

[17] *Nation*, CXLIX (September 23, 1939), 307–308.
[18] Winston Churchill, *Their Finest Hour* (Boston, 1949), 404.

Chat" to the country on December 29, 1940, the President warned that a massive American production of the tools of war was needed to sustain Great Britain and help prevent the threat which a German victory would pose for the United States. "We must be the great arsenal of democracy. For this is an emergency as serious as war itself." [19] To implement this idea, Roosevelt urged Congress to make available by sale, loan, or lease virtually any war material to any nation whose defense the President might deem vital to the United States. The Lend-Lease Act of March 11, 1941, which resulted from Roosevelt's suggestion, carried the United States about as far as it was possible to go short of actual war. "Peace through war by proxy," was Senator Vandenberg's sarcastic description of the measure which "drove the final nail into the coffin of neutrality." [20] When the United States then also assumed responsibility for patrolling the Western Atlantic and for convoying war material more than halfway to Britain, it was obvious that the country had moved from its position as an unneutral nonbelligerent to that of a full partner in an undeclared war.

Although the President was careful to request support for such measures as the Lend-Lease legislation in terms of the defense and security of the United States, he did not yield the ideal of American world leadership. "On the face of it," as Robert Osgood points out, "Roosevelt's idea of turning the nation into an arsenal of democracy was the most extreme interpretation of the American mission, in terms of a tangible commitment, ever suggested by anyone charged with the conduct of America's foreign affairs." [21]

After the fall of France in 1940 the American people believed, to a much greater extent than in 1917, that their own national security was at stake. Historians accordingly have given considerable weight to realistic considerations of self-interest as a major factor in explaining America's entrance into the Second World War. Such national self-interest was also compatible with the essentially negative aspects of United States foreign policy—the isolationist desire

[19] *Peace and War*, 607.

[20] *The Private Papers of Senator Vandenberg*, A. H. Vandenberg, Jr., ed. (Boston, 1952), 8; R. W. Leopold, *The Growth of American Foreign Policy* (New York, 1962), 570.

[21] R. E. Osgood, *Ideals and Self-Interest in America's Foreign Relations* (Chicago, 1953), 417.

for neutrality and the general American unwillingness to seek genuinely international solutions to the world's fundamental economic and political problems. But the continued Rooseveltian stress on national defense exaggerated the extent to which the security of the United States was threatened, except in the important sense in which American interests had become worldwide. What was at stake, in actuality, was not the popular notion of the military defense of the United States and its possessions, but the much broader question of whether the United States through participation in World War II would be able to assume the international role for which it had been preparing since at least the turn of the century. Only official American entrance into the war would enable the United States to take a commanding lead in shaping the coming postwar world. By 1941 it was therefore clear that, while the United States was making every effort to sustain Great Britain and restrain Japan, it was also fashioning a blueprint of the future based on the assumption of American belligerency and victory in the Great War.

Early in 1941, in his Four Freedoms Address and later in the Atlantic Charter, Roosevelt announced plans for world leadership which were largely a mixture of the New Deal and Wilson's Fourteen Points. In his annual message to Congress of January 6, 1941, he asserted:

In the future days, which we seek to make secure, we look forward to a world founded upon four essential freedoms.

The first is freedom of speech and expression—everywhere in the world.

The second is freedom of every person to worship God in his own way—everywhere in the world.

The fourth is freedom from fear—which, translated into world terms, means economic understandings which will secure to every nation a healthy peacetime life for its inhabitants—everywhere in the world.

The fourth freedom is fear—which, translated into world terms, means a world-wide reduction of armaments to such a point and in such a thorough fashion that no nation will be in a position to commit an act of physical aggression against any neighbor—anywhere in the world.[22]

22 *Peace and War*, 611.

The Atlantic Charter was a result of the secret meeting in August, 1941, off the Newfoundland Coast of the American President and the British Prime Minister Winston Churchill. Amid rumors of still further steps along the American road to war, to make possible greater United States cooperation with the British in the North Atlantic and in the South Pacific, the two statesmen discussed plans for the eventual peace. Almost as an afterthought, and at first in the form of a news release rather than as a formal signed document, Roosevelt and Churchill agreed to a joint declaration setting forth the common aims of the United States and the United Kingdom:

First, their countries seek no aggrandizement, territorial or other;

Second, they desire to see no territorial changes that do not accord with the freely expressed wishes of the peoples concerned;

Third, they respect the right of all peoples to choose the form of government under which they will live; and they wish to see sovereign rights and self-government restored to those who have been forcibly deprived of them;

Fourth, they will endeavor, with due respect for their existing obligations, to further the enjoyment by all states, great or small, victor or vanquished, of access, on equal terms, to the trade and to the raw materials of the world . . . ;

Fifth, they desire to bring about the fullest collaboration between all nations in the economic field with the object of securing, for all, improved labor standards, economic advancement, and social security;

Sixth, after the final destruction of the Nazi tyranny, they hope to see established a peace which will afford to all nations the means of dwelling in safety within their own boundaries, and which will afford assurance that all men in all lands may live out their lives in freedom from fear and want;

Seventh, such a peace should enable all men to traverse the high seas and oceans without hindrance;

Eighth, they believe that all of the nations of the world, for realistic as well as spiritual reasons, must come to the abandonment of the use of force. . . .[23]

The Atlantic charter, as a mutual Anglo-American pronouncement issued in the context of the fast-changing developments in the War in the second half of 1941, was an implied promise of American belligerency. Whenever that occurred, America in conjunction with

[23] *Ibid.*, 718–719.

Britain proposed to exercise joint leadership in policing the world. Although Soviet Russia after the German invasion in June, 1941, became a full partner in the War upon the Nazis, its role as well as that of China was less clear in terms of future planning for peace on a global scale. Despite the growing wartime expressions of Soviet-American friendship after 1941, there remained considerable suspicion and antagonism on the part of each nation. Earlier the Soviet pact with Hitler and the Russo-Finnish War had increased the traditional American fears and dislike of communism, while the Soviets, in turn, could not forget America's intervention and non-recognition policies after the First World War. Yet a purely Anglo-American peace program could not be considered realistic so long as Russian and Chinese land forces were doing the bulk of the fighting against the Axis. Effective plans and decisions, therefore, would have to have the approval of the so-called Big Three or Big Four—including Russia, and perhaps China, as well as Great Britain and the United States. Moreover, when the Soviets were able to turn back the Nazi invaders, they were also able to make demands and seek safeguards for the security of their frontiers which were hardly compatible with the Atlantic Charter's repudiation of any political or territorial changes in the prewar status of Eastern Europe.

Meanwhile, as the United States itself moved closer to war, lend-lease was extended to Russia, and the American navy began the active protection and convoying of war materials across the North Atlantic. Clashes between American destroyers and Nazi submarines indicated that the shooting had begun in advance of the war and that full-scale hostilities could not be long delayed. In regard to Japan and possible war in the Pacific, the earlier United States embargo on munitions and strategic materials was followed on July 26, 1941, by an order freezing all Japanese assets in the United States. While American opinion continued to view a threatened Japanese advance in Southeast Asia as a menace secondary to the situation in Europe, it seemed probable that the United States might enter the War against the Axis by way of the back door of the Pacific.

In terms of trade and investments in the Far East, United States commitments in China were vastly less important than the American economic stake in Japan. As Secretary Hull pointed out in 1938, however, the American concern over China transcended the actual realities of its financial interest. American foreign policy, he declared, was part of a "much broader and much more fundamental interest—which is, that orderly processes in international relationships . . . be maintained." [24] Seen in this light, the major concern of American policy makers was whether the American people would support a war to protect the status quo in the Far East if the Japanese did not directly attack the Philippines or other American possessions. On December 7, 1941, the Japanese assault on Pearl Harbor resolved this dilemma as well as the problem of waiting for the shooting war with the Nazis on the Atlantic to become a declared war.

The Japanese air attack on Pearl Harbor came as the culmination of a long series of steps in which the United States by a "hard" policy of increasing economic pressure had sought to contain Japanese expansion in China and the Far East. From the Japanese standpoint its interests and ambitions in Eastern Asia were little different than those which the United States had traditionally exercised in Latin America. Pearl Harbor therefore was the Japanese response to what they felt was America's unjustified challenge. On the much-debated Allied question of whether the Roosevelt Administration had tried to maneuver the Japanese into firing the first shot, perhaps the soundest judgment is that of Richard Current, who has expressed the view that American leaders had no intention of waiting for a Japanese attack on American territory nor of compelling an attack on Pearl Harbor. Instead, if the Japanese proceeded southward against the British and Dutch possessions in Southeast Asia, the American policy makers proposed two ways of enabling the United States to act. "One was a diplomatic 'maneuver,' a warning to Japan; and the other a political 'maneuver,' a message to Congress and the people. Both the dispatch to Japan and the address to Congress were to be phrased in such a way that, if the Japanese proceeded with their southward movement, even though they did not touch any American territory, they would nevertheless appear to be deliberately assailing our vital interests and, in that sense, attacking *us.*" [25]

24 *Ibid.*, 416.
25 R. N. Current, "How Stimson Meant to 'Maneuver' the Japanese," *Mississippi Valley Historical Review*, XL (June, 1953), 74.

With war a fact there was general American agreement with Secretary of War Stimson's confession that his "first feeling was of relief that the indecision was over and that a crisis had come in a way which would unite all our people." [26] On January 1, 1942, the new role of the United States was formalized with the announcement in Washington of the Declaration of the United Nations, signed by the representatives of the twenty-six countries at war with the Axis. Subscribing to the principles of the Atlantic Charter, each nation pledged itself to employ its full resources in the war "and not to make a separate armistice or peace with the enemies." [27] Although the details of the United Nations remained to be worked out, the Declaration was important not only as a pledge of wartime unity in the fight against the Axis but also because it provided the embryo of a new world organization for peace. Significantly, in the light of America's rejection of the Treaty of Versailles in 1919, Congress in the Connally-Fulbright resolutions signified its approval at the earliest practicable date of the establishment of "a general international organization, based on the principles of the sovereign equality of all peace-loving states, and open to membership by all such states, large and small, for the maintenance of international peace and security." [28]

Pending the outcome of the war and the realization of the peace, the Grand Alliance of the United States, Great Britain, and the Soviet Union, together with China in the Far East, found it difficult to translate popular enthusiasms into definite commitments for the future. By postponing the consideration of certain controversial questions which might have interfered with the successful prosecution of the war, Washington officials undoubtedly hoped that the unity forged in victory would become the basis of an acceptable and enduring peace. Moreover, as American policy makers understood, Congress, although it had agreed in principle with the concept of the United Nations, might well prove reluctant to ratify specific bargains made by the leaders of the Big Three or Four nations. For example, neither Congress nor the Administration

[26] H. L. Stimson and McGeorge Bundy, *On Active Service in Peace and War* (New York, 1948), 393.

[27] *Peace and War*, 851.

[28] *A Decade of American Foreign Policy, Basic Documents, 1941–49*, U.S. Senate Committee on Foreign Relations, ed. (Washington, 1950), 14.

could neglect the political influence of the several million Americans of Eastern European origins who remained intensely hostile to any expansion of the old prewar Russian boundaries at the expense of the smaller countries from the Baltic to the Black Sea.

For the most part, therefore, the work of the wartime conferences of the Heads of State and their foreign secretaries was shrouded in secrecy. This was partly because of military necessities, but it was also frequently necessary to conceal the growing split between the East and the West. On such important matters as the timing of the Second Front in Europe and the future status of Eastern Europe, Russia, Great Britain, and the United States were far from united. And even the widely publicized, and also subsequently much criticized, Roosevelt call at Casablanca in January, 1943, for the unconditional surrender of Germany was to be understood mainly as an Anglo-American pledge to Russia of no separate peace on the part of the West. Later at Cairo, Chiang Kai-shek and the Chinese received this same kind of assurance for the War against Japan.

Despite the widespread optimism of the American public during the War years, it was plain that the task of building a lasting peace would be beset with many difficulties. Neither the enthusiastic rhetoric of President Roosevelt's wartime speeches nor the idealistic visions of Wendell Willkie's *One World* and Henry Wallace's *Century of the Common Man* provided a realistic insight into the troubled nature of the Grand Alliance. Certainly it was naïve to expect that the principles of the Four Freedoms and the Atlantic Charter could be automatically achieved through the War. Total war by its very nature was at odds with the concept of a reasonable peace. And in the wartime coalition of the United Nations, the Big Three were often held together by little more than their common resistance to German expansion. Clearly, as Norman Graebner points out,

an Anglo-American victory in World War II, similar to that achieved in 1918, was prejudiced even before the entry of the United States into the war. Having been obliged because of military weakness to align themselves with one of the world's leading dictatorships, the two nations were bound to this alliance at the peace table. Unfortunately, their victorious ally did not share their values or their limited interests in re-creating the prewar balance of power, modified only by the imposition of some military and political restrictions on the defeated nations. Whatever the ultimate success of British and American arms, Europe's fate was no longer a matter to be determined solely by the great democracies of the West.[29]

At Teheran and Yalta the popular American expectations of a future international Utopia dominated by the United States were incompatible with the wartime facts of diplomacy which Roosevelt and Churchill had to face when they negotiated with Stalin. The agreements by which the Big Three hoped to conclude the War and make good the peace were later unfairly denounced in the United States as being responsible for the loss of Poland and of Nationalist China by the West. But it was obvious that Russia and China also would have to share prominently in making the decisions that would govern the postwar world. And, especially in regard to Eastern Europe, it was certain that despite the arrangements for governments "broadly representative of all democratic elements" made at the conference table, the Soviet Union would assert its special interests and desire for security. For the sake of both Russia and the West and their mutual victory in the War, it was desirable that the Yalta Agreement preserve as much unity as possible. To this end, therefore, the intentionally vague and ambiguous Yalta Charter provided:

I   A World Organization
II   The Liberation of Europe
III   The Dismemberment of Germany
IV   The Military Occupation and Control of Germany with a Zone of Occupation for the French
V   Reparations from Germany
VI   The Trial of Major War Criminals
VII   A Poland with an eastern boundary generally along the 1919 Curzon line, and a Provisional Government "pledged to the holding of free and unfettered elections as soon as possible on the basis of universal suffrage and secret ballot."

Declarations for other countries occupied by the Axis were almost as controversial and ambiguous as those for Poland, but provision was made for future meetings of the British, Russian, and United States Foreign Secretaries. Finally, in a Secret Agreement Regarding Japan, the Soviet Union in return for the restoration of territories

29 N. A. Graebner, *Ideas and Diplomacy* (New York, 1964), 637.

lost to Japan in 1904 agreed to enter the war in the Pacific "in two or three months after Germany has surrendered and the war in Europe has terminated." [30]

In terms of completing the War and organizing the United Nations, Yalta was a success. And even its most celebrated failure—its inability to carry out the provision for a Free Poland—was not immediately apparent. If, as seemed the case, Russia had agreed to principles of self-determination in Eastern Europe which she had no intention to respect, at least the Soviet approval of the Yalta Charter indicated a desire to avoid an open break with the West. It is a question, moreover, whether Roosevelt and Churchill were wise, for the sake of their own national political interests, to pressure Stalin into making concessions that were essentially contrary to Russian national interests and which were thus all the more likely to be broken. Despite the depth of the disagreements at Yalta, however, and the face-saving nature of the Charter for all three leaders, it seemed true that in the United States, as Harry Hopkins later recalled:

> We really believed in our hearts that this was the dawn of the new day we had all been praying for and talking about for so many years. We were absolutely certain that we had won the first great victory of the peace—and by "we," I *mean* all of us, the whole civilized human race. The Russians had proved that they could be reasonable and farseeing and there wasn't any doubt in the minds of the President or any of us that we could live with them and get along with them peacefully for as far into the future as any of us could imagine.[31]

As the greatest war in history finally drew to a close in 1945, it appeared highly probable that one of its results would be to unleash new revolutionary forces of which there was in the West only an incomplete popular comprehension. The American people, supremely confident of America's strength at the close of the War, were ill-prepared to accept any forthcoming challenge to United States world leadership. Official Washington had not equipped the nation to understand Nationalist China's basic weakness or to deal with Soviet strength. Instead, in the fervor of their recent conversion from isolationism to internationalism, the American public were all

---

[30] *A Decade of American Foreign Policy,* 27–34.
[31] Quoted in Sherwood, *Roosevelt and Hopkins,* 870.

too frequently blind to the fact that their own new views often only projected older nationalistic prejudices upon a world stage. Moreover the Grand Alliance of the United Nations against the Axis was, in itself, despite the rhetoric of collective security, sometimes "hard to distinguish from the timeworn statecraft of alliances designed to achieve for their adherents some kind of 'balance,' which usually meant predominance." [32]

Yet in 1945, despite the evident difficulties, America's political commitment to the concept of the United Nations and its vast economic and military role in the recent hostilities gave every assurance that the United States would continue to exercise a large measure of world leadership in the years ahead. This national determination to assume the burdens of responsibility and the privileges of power had become the most important factor underlying the entire foreign policy of the United States. United States diplomacy in the postwar world accordingly was to be understood in terms of this American effort to maintain its preeminent position in the midst of the challenges of the Cold War. With all of its enormous potential for good or ill, the explosion of the first atomic bombs over Japan in August, 1945, symbolized the fact of America's dominance. But the overwhelming final defeat of the Axis nations was only the first test of the unity of the United Nations and of America's own tremendous new role in the postwar world.

SELECTED REFERENCES

Beard, Charles A. *President Roosevelt and the Coming of the War, 1941.* New Haven: Yale University Press, 1948.

Drummond, Donald F. *The Passing of American Neutrality, 1937–1941.* Ann Arbor: University of Michigan Press, 1955.

Gardner, Lloyd C. *Economic Aspects of New Deal Diplomacy.* Madison: University of Wisconsin Press, 1964.

Hogan, Willard N. *International Conflict and Collective Security.* Lexington: University of Kentucky Press, 1955.

Langer, William L. and S. E. Gleason. *The Challenge to Isolation, 1937–1940.* New York: Harper, 1952.

[32] R. N. Current, "The United States and 'Collective Security,'" in *Isolation and Security*, Alexander DeConde, ed. (Durham, N.C., 1957), 55.

————. *The Undeclared War, 1940–1941*. New York: Harper, 1953.

Neumann, William L. *America Encounters Japan: From Perry to Mac-Arthur*. Baltimore: Johns Hopkins Press, 1963.

————. *Making the Peace, 1941–1945: The Diplomacy of the Wartime Conferences*. Washington: Foundation for Foreign Affairs, 1950.

Snell, John L., ed. *The Meaning of Yalta: Big Three Diplomacy and the New Balance of Power*. Baton Rouge: Louisiana State University Press, 1956.

Stromberg, Roland N. *Collective Security and American Foreign Policy: From the League of Nations to Nato*. New York: Praeger, 1963.

Tansill, Charles C. *Back Door to War: The Roosevelt Foreign Policy, 1933–1941*. Chicago: Regnery, 1952.

Weller, George. *Bases Overseas: An American Trusteeship in Power*. New York: Harcourt, Brace, 1944.

IX

Containment and Cold War

American foreign policy following World War II was conditioned primarily by the rapid deterioration in relations between the Western Allies and the Soviet Union. Although the policy of containment and the so-called Cold War were consequences of the Second World War, this unhappy state of international affairs was not what most Americans had hoped to see come out of the long struggle against the Axis powers. During the war, in the Atlantic Charter, in the Declaration of the United Nations, and in the Agreement at Yalta, the United States had assumed that it could deal with Russia and control the peace. Roosevelt and American political leaders were, on the whole, more confident than Churchill and British officials that the various differences between the Soviet Union and the West might be reconciled in the personal diplomacy of the Big Three. By taking on the role of mediator between the declining fortunes of the British Empire and the rising star of the Soviets, President Roosevelt no doubt believed that the United States was carrying out its mission of global leadership and that America would be able to dominate the future destinies of the postwar world.

The contrast between the generally optimistic American wartime expectations and the underlying diplomatic realities which emerged after 1945 again led to the pessimistic conclusion that the United States had won the war only to lose the peace. Partly as a reaction to this growing feeling of popular disillusionment American policy makers, in turn, were determined to maintain United States strength and to confront the Soviet postwar challenge to American world leadership. In one of his first major addresses on foreign policy President Truman, at the Navy Day celebration in New York City in October, 1945, asserted that the United States sought no territorial gains "Outside of the right to establish necessary bases for our own protection. . . . The atomic bomb," the President declared, "does not alter the basic foreign policy of the United States. . . . But when our demobilization is all finished as planned, the United States will still be the greatest naval power on earth. In addition to that naval power," he pointed out, "we shall have one of the most powerful air forces in the world. And just the other day, so that on short notice we could mobilize a powerful and well-equipped land, sea, and air force, I asked the Congress to adopt universal training." [1]

Influenced by the cult of power politics and accepting the philosophy of peace by force, the United States after the War moved to establish a chain of air bases and military posts overseas, while American opinion opposed further concessions to what was regarded as the ambitious and aggressively expansionist nature of the policies of the Soviet Union. "By 1950," Selig Adler has written, "the United States had returned not to the isolation of Warren Harding, but rather to the *Realpolitik* of Theodore Roosevelt. . . . Our postwar diplomacy thus bore a closer resemblance to the statecraft of Prince Metternich and Bismarck than to the doctrines of Presidents Wilson and F. D. Roosevelt." [2]

In the period following World War II, United States diplomacy operated on the twin premises that (1) the state of international affairs, described after 1947 by the term Cold War, was to be a more or less chronic condition, and that (2) the sources of Soviet strength would have to be met by the unceasing vigilance and superior counterforce of the United States and its Western Allies. Only on these assumptions of the protracted hostility of the Soviet Communist world with that of the Western nations were American Cold War and containment policies at all understandable. And, at the same time, it was of course also true that in a world so divided the earlier visions of One World of United Nations were fast reduced to a noble dream for some still-distant Utopia.

Within the bipolarized world which took form after 1945, the

[1] *Public Papers of the Presidents, Harry S. Truman, 1945* (Washington, 1961), 431–438.

[2] Selig Adler, *The Isolationist Impulse* (New York, 1957), 379, 429.

United States and the Soviet Union, despite the latter's staggering losses during the war, were incomparably the two greatest nation-states or empires. No other country had the industrial might or the armed forces to vie with the disciplined manpower of the Soviet Union, the atomic bomb of the United States, or the vast scientific and economic resources of both powers. No other nation equalled the United States or the Soviet Union in their pragmatic and technological abilities to control the forces of both man and nature. And finally, no other national state seemed able to generate a body of ideas comparable to the revolutionary impact and worldwide influence of the ideologies of Russian communism and American democracy.

In contrast to the situation after the First World War, when Russia and the United States retreated into political isolationism, the diplomatic concerns of each country now extended around the globe. The United States, for example, proposed to keep relatively large occupation forces in Germany and Japan, while at the same time it developed plans for expanding American air bases at strategic points throughout the world. Unlike the 1920's, when neither Russia nor the United States was a member of the League of Nations—unwilling and willing exiles—both countries now asserted leadership over their respective blocs of allies and satellites. Thus, instead of being a neutralist third force, poised between the two groups of the satisfied and the dissatisfied nations, the United States and the Soviet Union after World War II stood as rivals in a global contest for economic power and political supremacy. Western Europe, weakened by its struggle with Nazi Germany, lost its traditional world role, while the peoples of Asia and Africa were as yet only beginning to emerge as modern national states. Both Russia and the United States, therefore, were able to move into the power vacuum created by the Second World War.

Although the origins of the Soviet-American conflict were rooted in history—and particularly in the experience of the two World Wars—the new opportunities for world power and leadership open to each nation after 1945 were in themselves a large part of the explanation of their growing antagonism. Thus the traditional American fears of communism were heightened by the increase of Russian territory and influence as a result of the war. And the Soviets, in turn, were understandably reluctant to accept United

States world leadership and the substitution of a *pax Americana*, utilizing air power and the atomic bomb, for the older nineteenth-century enforcement of international law and order by the British navy. With the destruction of the Nazi armies, the wartime unity imposed by exigencies of the common struggle against Hitler's Germany came to an end. And, although the United Nations was convened as planned at San Francisco less than two weeks after President Roosevelt's death, the Big Three were no longer able to conceal their real differences by the formulation of new Yalta Agreements. Between the termination of the Second World War and the swift onset of the Cold War there was accordingly no real peace, but only a delayed public awareness of this bitter fact.

For the San Francisco Conference at which the Charter of the United Nations was drafted, Roosevelt before his death had done his utmost to avoid the mistakes of 1918 and to insure bipartisan American political support for the new international organization. This was easier for Roosevelt and his successor Harry Truman than for Wilson, in large part because the Conference had only the responsibility for establishing the United Nations, while the adoption of permanent World War II peace treaties was left in the hands of the belligerents. The most serious controversy at the Conference, the question of the extent of the veto to be exercised by the great powers in the Security Council, was resolved finally by a direct personal appeal to Stalin. The United States had strongly opposed the Soviet proposal to use the veto as a procedural technique to prevent important international issues from being discussed in the Security Council. No doubt American policy makers expected that free debate in the U.N. would provide a basis for submitting Soviet conduct to the forum of world public opinion. On matters of substance calling for action by the U.N., however, the United States as much as Russia favored the big-power veto. Retention of the veto by the United States was, after all, the best means of forestalling the type of isolationist objections which the Senate had raised to American participation in the League of Nations and the World Court.

In respect to the other controversial issues at San Francisco, the United States was likewise successful in securing Soviet agreement. By the device of a Trusteeship Council, the American Republic was able to retain possession of Japanese islands in the Pacific, and it also gained acceptance for the inclusion of regional pacts within the framework of the United Nations Charter. Thus the Organization of American States and later the North Atlantic Treaty Organization were capable of being reconciled with the United States' obligations to the U.N. In retrospect it is not unfair to say that the United States generally had its way at San Francisco and that, whatever its strengths or weaknesses, the Charter of the United Nations was largely the creature of the United States and of the preliminary planning of the Allied experts at Dumbarton Oaks. Moreover, despite Russia's subsequent liberal use of the veto in the Security Council, the basic lines of decision in the U.N. seldom deviated very much from the overall goals of American foreign policy.

At Potsdam, after the San Francisco Conference, the Heads of State of the Big Three had their last wartime meeting in order to make plans for postwar control of defeated Germany and for the final victory over Japan. Officially the United States was still anxious that Russia honor its Yalta pledge to enter the Far Eastern conflict from two to three months after the defeat of Hitler. At Potsdam, however, although no peace treaty could be worked out for Germany, President Truman was able to disclose to Premier Stalin the important news that American scientists had successfully developed a new weapon of unusual force. This information may have come as no great surprise to the Soviet leader, but it affected significantly the timetable of the war in the Pacific as well as the whole context of Soviet-American relations. Possession of the bomb gave added scientific and military assurance to American foreign policy and strengthened American claims to world leadership. Meanwhile the decision to use the bomb in the Pacific theater, and the haste to explode it over Hiroshima without any prior public demonstration of its effectiveness, seem to have been based in part on a United States desire to complete the war against Japan before Russia's expected entry. Thus American pressure to get the Soviets at the Yalta Conference to agree to fight against the Japanese in China—a policy based on mistaken United States military intelligence estimates of the duration and difficulty of the war in the Pacific—reacted to

America's own disadvantage. In a complete change of national attitudes on the part of each country, Russia made haste to enter the very last stages of a war which the United States suddenly desired to finish by itself.

America's questionable and controversial resort to the bomb for its own war purposes, and the evident intention of the Truman Administration to keep atomic energy as a "sacred trust," had fateful international and domestic implications. Signifying distrust of Russia, it also quite naturally intensified Soviet fears of American power. The decision likewise largely ignored the counter-recommendation of Secretary of War Stimson that the United States enter at once into direct negotiation with Russia for the purpose of working out some method for the international control of atomic energy. Stimson, who had played an important role in encouraging the research that had led to the bomb and who had also advocated its use against Japan was, without regretting those decisions, nevertheless most anxious that the United States try every possible means to reach an agreement with Russia in the whole area of nuclear energy. He knew that reputable scientists discounted the possibility that America's exclusive knowledge of the bomb could long be kept secret. Even temporary sole possession of so powerful a weapon greatly increased American fears of espionage, however, and the exposure of a Russian spy ring operating in Canada, and the ensuing disclosures of Communist spying in the United States, did much to arouse public opinion against a conciliatory foreign policy.

Anxious to protect its vested interest in atomic energy, but also uneasy over the way in which the bomb had been used against Japan, the United States sought some means of international control which would not at the same time jeopardize its own national security. The obvious and overwhelming potential worldwide significance of atomic energy encouraged general support for the decision of the General Assembly of the United Nations to establish a commission to formulate plans for its international development and control. This commission endorsed a United States proposal, drafted by Bernard Baruch and David Lilienthal, that an international administrative body be created with monopolistic controls and full powers of inspection to insure against any nation's unilateral exploitation of atomic energy for destructive purposes. Upon the establishment of such a U.N. commission, the United States would stop making bombs and turn over, or destroy, its existing stocks of nuclear weapons. Russia, however, called for the immediate destruction and outlawing of the bomb as well as the right to veto decisions of the commission. Unwilling to expose their totalitarian society to open inspection, and dependent upon American good faith in revealing its secret of producing the bomb, the Soviets were also fearful that their minority position in the United Nations might subject them to the unfair discrimination of any international body.

While the Soviets were asking the United States to relinquish whatever scientific and military advantages it enjoyed, the United States, in turn, was reluctant to give up its unilateral possession of the bomb until adequate international safeguards, not subject to Russian veto, were assured. Actually, with the exercise of good faith on the part of both nations, either the Soviet or the American plan could have worked. Moreover, many American scientists, believing that Russia would soon be able to produce its own bombs, questioned the value of the whole United States policy of secrecy. In any case a Russian veto of the decisions of a U.N. control comission was not likely to do more than announce publicly the fact that international cooperation in atomic energy policy had broken down. This, rather than the veto, would be the real danger to the United States and the rest of the world.

So long as the United States retained its initial advantage in developing nuclear power, some American leaders presumably were not disappointed that Russia had rejected the Baruch-Lilienthal plan of international control. In the long run, however, as the Soviets made their own great scientific advances and as other nations, too, were able to carry out successful test explosions, it seemed all too probable that the world had lost its first best opportunity to avoid an international arms race in the field of atomic weapons. Although America's planners made sole possession of the bomb a prime adjunct of United States foreign policy and a major deterrent with which to counter Soviet land forces in Europe, this advantage was illusory. World opinion would hardly have sanctioned use of the bomb, and in any case its one-sided effect would be lost whenever the Russians achieved their own nuclear weapons. Moreover, if it was really America's nuclear power which held the Russians at bay in Europe, as Churchill and others contended, it could well be asked why this great source of strength did not enable the United States and the Western Allies to negotiate a favorable peace settlement with the Soviets.

Instead the impasse between Russia and the West over the international control of atomic energy was paralleled by the breakdown of the Big Three's postwar plans for a peace settlement in Europe. It is true that the most notorious of the German Nazi leaders were sentenced to death or imprisonment at the Allied War Crimes Trials in Nuremberg, while peace treaties were also eventually signed with Finland, Hungary, Bulgaria, Rumania, Italy, and Austria. But in the cases of Poland and Germany, Russia and the West were far from agreement.

Despite the promises at Yalta for the establishment of a free Polish government of all factions, it became obvious that in Eastern Europe the Soviets were unwilling to risk the creation of hostile regimes through the democratic process of free elections. In an area recently liberated and still occupied by the Red armies, the Soviet Union was determined that the new governments would be Communist in their essential policies and sympathies. Any extension of communism across Europe would, of course, endanger friendly relations with the Western Allies, especially if the latter persisted in their conservative policy of attempting to restore Europe to its pre-Hitler status. Whatever the risks to the Grand Alliance of the Big Three, however, Russia could hardly have been expected to yield what it felt were its historic national interests in Eastern Europe, although as a matter of fact the Soviet regime, unlike its Czarist predecessors, did not absorb Poland or Finland within its own national boundaries. Just as the United States sought to insure its defensive position in the Pacific Ocean by retaining former Japanese islands there, so the Soviet Union desired to secure its western frontier from another German invasion. For the West to try to force a settlement in Eastern Europe was, therefore, as Walter Lippmann pointed out,

a gigantic blunder, made by men who had had no part in the strategic conduct of the war, and failed to take into account its strategic consequences. For it narrowed the issue between Russia and the West to the very region where the conflict was sharpest and a settlement the most difficult.[3]

In a world in which many peoples were demanding radical changes and looking to Russia for leadership, the Soviet Union could not readily surrender the strong political and military position which it had achieved at great cost in Eastern Europe. Abdication there would have been tantamount to giving up its revolutionary heritage and all prospects of the eventual triumph of communism. Because of their vigorous dissent from this Russian goal, Americans were unwilling to accept the possibility that Stalin and the Soviet leaders were under as much compulsion as other world statesmen to defend and advance their political and economic system. The propaganda of the expansion of communism, even when hopeless, was as important to Russia as the concept of the Free World, even when it embraced countries ruled by military dictators, was to the United States. All too often, however, Americans fell into the error of confusing the bombastic Soviet rhetoric of international communism with Russia's traditional and limited objectives as a national state. The legitimate and largely successful resistance to the first of these goals was accordingly sometimes hurt by the unwise consistent United States opposition to the second.

Almost alone among top-rank American political figures, Secretary of Commerce and former Vice President Henry A. Wallace questioned the "get tough with Russia" policy of the Truman administration. In a memo to the President dated July 23, 1946, but not made public until September 17, Wallace urged the development in cooperation with the Soviets of practical plans for the two countries to live together in the same world without the danger of atomic war. Then on September 12, in the speech in New York which led to his resignation although it had been cleared in advance with President Truman, Wallace called upon the United States to match its professions of peace with action and deeds:

The real peace treaty we now need is between the United States and Russia. On our part, we should recognize that we have no more business in the *political* affairs of Eastern Europe than Russia has in the *political* affairs of Latin America, Western Europe and the United States. . . .

[3] Walter Lippmann, "A Year of Peacemaking," *Atlantic Monthly*, CLXXVIII (December, 1946), 36.

As for Germany, we all must recognize that an equitable settlement, based on a unified German nation, is absolutely essential to any lasting European settlement. . . .

Meanwhile, the Russians should stop teaching that their form of communism must, by force if necessary, untimately triumph over democratic capitalism—while we should close our ears to those among us who would have us believe that Russian communism and our free enterprise system cannot live, one with another, in a profitable and productive peace.[4]

Wallace's plea for a thorough-going agreement and conciliation of interests between America and the Soviet Union, although he carried it into the Presidential campaign of 1948, ran counter to the course of events in Europe and the United States. However remote the supposed ultimate triumph of world communism, the leaders of Western Europe and the United States were convinced that in its weakened postwar state Europe was prey to the pressures of Communist revolutions at home and to the threat of Russian expansion from abroad. Without America's financial help, it was widely believed that the war-torn Continent would be unable to regain its former industrial power and achieve some semblance of political and social stability. Responding to these fears and acting on these assumptions, the United States offered its Truman Doctrine, Marshall Plan, and North Atlantic Treaty Organization as major steps in a program for containing the spread of communism. The protective shield of the Monroe Doctrine was now being widened to include the whole world outside the Soviet Union.

The Truman Doctrine especially, though it seemed to sweep away all remaining vestiges of American isolationism, was in fact an announcement of a nationalistic, interventionist foreign policy for the United States. A year after Winston Churchill's sensational "iron curtain" speech at Fulton, Missouri, in March, 1946, which had served as a trial balloon in the Cold War, the Truman Doctrine brought into the open the covert trends of American diplomacy and public opinion. In forceful language and in an atmosphere akin to a war crisis, President Truman called upon Congress for four hundred million dollars to enable the United States to take over British

[4] H. A. Wallace, *The Fight for Peace* (New York, 1946), 19–20.

strategic responsibilities in the Eastern Mediterranean. In approving economic and military aid to Greece and Turkey, the United States not only entered an area never before considered an American sphere of influence, but it also announced bluntly that the Cold War had indeed arrived.

Many Americans, indignant over the way in which President Truman had bypassed the United Nations, feared that the new United States diplomacy would increase the likelihood of war with the Soviet Union. Even George Kennan, the designated chief of the State Department's Policy Planning Staff, seems to have been deeply disturbed by the harsh, uncompromising tone of the Truman Doctrine, and especially "the portraying of two opposing ways of life, and the open-end commitment to aid free peoples. . . ." [5] Kennan in earlier despatches from the American Embassy in Moscow after the war had urged a firmer United States response to Soviet Russia. But there is evidence that Kennan, the famous Mr. X, the author of the influential article in *Foreign Affairs* on "The Sources of Soviet Conduct" and the reputed intellectual godfather of the containment policy, considered his ideas as essentially a milder way of dealing with the Soviets than the Truman Doctrine.

Later the so-called Marshall Plan, providing large-scale economic aid to Europe, though apparently a natural extension of the Truman Doctrine, did modify the latter's ideological and military overtones. Nevertheless the gradual transition in the American foreign aid program from economic to military help and the establishment of the North Atlantic Treaty Organization made it clear that the United States was assuming the major responsibility for the defense of Western Europe and the area around the Mediterranean Sea. Elsewhere in Europe, the United States in its ambitious plans for the containment of communism had to rely on the United Nations and on Russian goodwill. Thus the American people were confronted with the fact that Europe was divided for the forseeable future by the reality of Russian power as well as by the symbolism of Churchill's iron curtain.

At no place was the establishment of the two Europes more apparent and more significant than in Germany and Berlin, where the original military occupation zones were transformed into the Governments of the East and the West. The extent of the United States'

5 J. M. Jones, *The Fifteen Weeks* (New York, 1955), 155.

own commitment in Germany was demonstrated most dramatically in the spring of 1948 when the Soviet action in cutting off the ordinary supply routes to West Berlin was countered at great cost for more than a year by the Allied Airlift. Despite the tremendous effort needed to keep West Berlin alive economically, it is possible that neither the United States nor the Soviet Union was in any hurry to settle the currency dispute which had first touched off the Berlin blockade. A Big Three conference over Berlin would necessarily have involved the much broader questions of a German peace treaty and German unification, matters which neither Russia nor the Western Allies felt it to be in their interests to resolve at this time. A strong Germany might again dominate the Continent, while a policy of continued division would permit the maintenance of a European buffer zone between Russia and the West. East Germany accordingly became another satellite state within the Soviet orbit, while the West German Bonn Government was included within the European Recovery Program and the North Atlantic Treaty Organization. Thus by the close of the 1940's the rigid German division and the leadership by the United States and Russia over their respective halves of Europe were accomplished facts of the Cold War.

In Europe the Cold War policy of the two Germanies was part of a general stalemate in which, however, Russia avoided a showdown with the United States over Berlin and NATO and in which the Western Allies, in turn, accepted reluctantly the results of the Soviet supremacy in Eastern Europe. This institution of what might be called a period of watchful waiting was in line with the program outlined by George Kennan. An opponent of carrying on diplomacy "with threats or blustering or superfluous gestures of outward 'toughness,'" Kennan believed that "United States policy toward the Soviet Union must be that of a long-term, patient but firm and vigilant containment of Russian expansive tendencies." Basically Kennan's analysis rested on the assumption that the United States and the West were in a better position than the Communist states to survive the heavy political, economic, and psychological costs of a protracted Cold War. Ultimately through the continued pressures of containment, the Free World would be able to force modifications in the Soviet system, as well as Russian acceptance of American world leadership. Since the major burden of such a program would rest on the American people, Kennan concluded that containment would be a gauge of national quality. "The issue of Soviet-American relations," he wrote, "is in essence a test of the over-all worth of the United States as a nation among nations." [6]

Though Kennan's rather pretentious justification of the policy of containment was more cautious than much of the actual American diplomacy in the Cold War, it rested nevertheless on what Walter Lippmann called "a disbelief in the possibility of a settlement of the issues raised by this war." From Kennan's observations that we cannot expect "to enjoy political intimacy with the Soviet regime," and that we must "regard the Soviet Union as a rival, not a partner in the political arena," and that "there can be no appeal to common purposes," Lippmann wrote that he had "reached the conclusion that all we can do is to 'contain' Russia until Russia changes, ceases to be our rival, and becomes our partner." Such a verdict, Lippmann felt, was "quite unwarranted." The history of diplomacy, he declared, was "the history of relations among rival powers, which did not enjoy political intimacy, and did not respond to appeals to common purposes. Nevertheless," he noted, "there have been settlements. Some of them did not last very long. Some of them did." But Lippmann concluded: "For a diplomat to think that rival and unfriendly powers cannot be brought to a settlement is to forget what diplomacy is all about." [7]

In the long run events demonstrated that so negative a program as containment—neither peace nor war—was difficult to sustain. First the American people had to be convinced continually that any real peace with the existing Soviet regime was impossible. And secondly, they had to be persuaded to accept a sophisticated policy of limited victories since nuclear war was too dangerous and dubious to be a viable alternative. In practice, however, one result of containment was the encouragement of a holy crusade against communism. Anti-communism was useful as an emotional substitute for war and as a release from the frustrations of containment, but it was hardly an adequate replacement for peace. Under the exigencies of the Cold War, the United States became committed abroad to the same kind of permanent and universal interventionism which Charles de Gaulle, for one, had predicted as the outcome of the extreme Ameri-

---

[6] G. F. Kennan, "The Sources of Soviet Conduct" (1947), in his *American Diplomacy, 1900–1950* (Chicago, 1951), 117, 124.

[7] Walter Lippmann, *The Cold War* (New York, 1947), 60.

can reaction from isolationism. Meanwhile in Washington the hysteria of McCarthyism and the Federal loyalty-security program became the logical domestic concomitants of the containment policy.

Containment abroad and McCarthyism at home together forced American foreign policy into the continually negative posture of having to justify all actions in terms of their probable effect on Russia. In their fear of communism, Americans were even ready to accept the Marxist notion of an inevitable war between capitalism and communism. And, as one liberal observer noted, "Stalin has really conquered the United States in that he has completed its militarization and has frightened it to death." [8] Seeing the danger in an American foreign policy that attempted to explain every decision on the basis of strategic calculations of a possible war with Russia, Walter Lippmann complained: "This damnable obsession has gotten to the point where we can hardly send milk to babies abroad without explaining that this is an important action in our cold war with Russian communism." [9]

Under the containment policy the whole concept of foreign aid emerged as essentially another facet of the Cold War. Going beyond humanitarian ideals of relief and technical assistance to so-called underdeveloped and underprivileged nations and peoples, foreign aid became a part of the gigantic world struggle between the United States and the Soviet Union. Often it involved a kind of blackmail in which nations gained American aid by offering to associate themselves with United States Cold War policies. Thus the United States granted economic and military assistance abroad primarily to try to thwart Russian influence, or to curb native Communist movements. More significant, perhaps, than the dangers of American control over the recipients of the aid was the ease with which all sorts of governments were able to extort funds from nervous American statesmen. In the period after World War II, United States foreign assistance, which became increasingly military aid, reached an impressive total amount of over 100 billion dollars. This enormous sum, however,

[8] O. G. Villard, quoted in A. A. Ekirch, *The Decline of American Liberalism* (New York, 1955), 320.
[9] "Today and Tomorrow," *Washington Post*, June 1, 1950.

helped to maintain the postwar prosperity of the United States, since most of the foreign aid funds were allotted in the form of grants for the purchase of American goods.

The wide range and intensity of American fears over Soviet expansion and the menace of communism were all the more extraordinary because they developed in a period when the American Communist Party lost most of its membership and virtually all of its influence, and in a time when Russia itself made no territorial gains beyond its 1948 limits. Compared with the historic frontiers of Russia under the Czars, the boundaries of the Soviets were not unduly extended. It is also noteworthy that Premier Khrushchev, with a fine disregard for revolutionary logic, was fond of justifying Soviet foreign policy by identifying it with that of his Czarist predecessors. Moreover, in this same postwar period, the American empire was by no means stationary. To the historic continental domain of the nineteenth-century Republic with the later colonial additions resulting from the War with Spain, plus traditional spheres of influence in Latin America, there were now added the former Japanese islands in the Pacific and a wide range of military bases and missions stretching around the globe.

At the same time that the United States was building up its postwar military empire abroad, the large-scale spending for the Cold War was causing the American domestic economy to take on some of the features of a garrison state. In national budgets approaching 100 billion dollars a year, more than three quarters of the appropriated funds were war-related: for the armed forces, foreign aid, intelligence activities, veterans' pensions, and interest payments on the national debt. Out of his increasing concern over this Cold War expansion of American military influence on foreign and domestic policy, President Eisenhower in his Farewell Address added his own personal warning to the nation. Thus he lent the prestige of his voice and position to the protests of those who feared that the power of the postwar military-industrial complex could endanger the fundamental processes of American democracy.

The high costs of projecting containment into a worldwide military crusade against communism and the increasing difficulties which the United States faced in the Cold War were nowhere more apparent than in Asia. There, as in Africa, the revolt against European colonialism and the sense of rising expectations among newly awakened nationalities created considerable native sympathy and support for regimes that were basically socialist or communist in their political economies and ideologies. In a period in which Europe was able to escape war and the further spread of communism while it also made a spectacular economic recovery, Nationalist China suffered defeat by the Communists, and Korea, and then Vietnam, involved the United States in long-drawn-out and costly conflicts. New and wide-ranging commitments in the Far East also carried United States foreign policy far beyond all previous precedents for the extension of American spheres of interest abroad. The old question of whether the United States should pursue an "Asia first" policy appealed to latent nationalist and imperialist sentiment at home, and it also enlisted the sympathies of those groups which had firm religious and emotional ties to China.

According to the popular opinion of large numbers of Americans, Russia's dominance in Eastern Europe and the triumph of the forces of Mao Tse-tung in China were equally the products of an international Communist conspiracy and of the weaknesses or perfidy of American foreign policy. With Mao's decisive victory over Chiang Kai-shek and the flight of the Chinese government to Formosa in 1949, the United States' wartime policy of establishing China as the foremost power in the Far East collapsed completely. In the words of one scholar this "was an even greater disaster for American policy than Pearl Harbor, a disaster which nullified the military victories of American power in the Pacific, 1942-1945." [10] Until the last stages of the Chinese Communists' triumph, they had received little support from Russia—far less, for example, that what the United States gave to Chiang and the Nationalists. Whether Russia doubted Mao's eventual success or feared his future power, the Soviets appeared to be more concerned with extracting what profit they could in Manchuria and Korea from the ending of the war with Japan. To a great extent, therefore, Soviet Russia, like the United States and the West, seems to have miscalculated the deep, underlying strength of the new revolutionary forces in China—

[10] W. L. Neumann, *America Encounters Japan* (Baltimore, 1963), 306.

a nucleus of power which, as subsequent events demonstrated, was growing constantly in strength.

Despite the substantial pressures for some kind of American military intervention to help Chiang Kai-shek return to the Chinese mainland, the major crisis in the Far Eastern policy of the United States came in Korea. There President Truman's decision to resist the North Korean invasion and to enlist the support of the United Nations, in what was somewhat euphemistically considered a police action, imbued American foreign policy with the crusading spirit that characterized the containment program in Europe. But the inability of the Truman administration to bring the long-drawn-out Korean War to a satisfactory conclusion disillusioned the American people and added to the illiberal pressures of McCarthyism at home.

Essentially the issue in Korea, dramatized by General MacArthur's eventual dismissal, was whether the war should be confined to the limited goals set by the United Nations or be broadened in such a way that it would risk a major conflict between the United States and Red China. Despite the widespread emotional backing in the United States for MacArthur's aggressive military tactics, more sober American opinion, strongly supported by Allied sentiment, was reflected in General Omar Bradley's testimony in the Senate hearings that the MacArthur strategy would "involve us in the wrong war, at the wrong place, at the wrong time, and with the wrong enemy." [11] This judgment also seemed to be substantiated when, in 1952, the American people elected Eisenhower President, in part, at least, because of his moderation and promise to go to Korea to help conclude what had become a highly unpopular struggle.

Although the Korean War was terminated by the Armistice of July 27, 1953, the experience remained a somewhat mixed example of the collective security policies of the United Nations. In Korea itself only a stalemate had been reached, while the Chinese Communists were embittered at the United States for its dominant role in the War and for its continued policy of refusing to have Red China voted a seat in the U.N. Moreover, the end of the War in Korea did not bring peace to the Far East. To counter the seemingly monolithic Communist bloc of Russia and Red China, the United

[11] Quoted in J. W. Spanier, *The Truman-MacArthur Controversy and the Korean War* (Cambridge, Mass., 1959), 247.

States committed itself, apart from the U.N., to an ever-increasing program of economic and military aid to countries on the periphery of the Chinese land mass which had been surrendered by Japan after World War II. Taking over from the French in Vietnam in 1954, the United States organized SEATO, a military alliance for the defense of Southeast Asia patterned on the example of NATO in Europe. Thus in Asia, as in Europe, most of the continent was divided in its allegiance between communism and what was perhaps optimistically termed the Free World. In the long run, it could be argued plausibly that Red China would be contained better by its own internal strengths or weaknesses than by American military alliances with reactionary governments too weak to maintain themselves without massive financial support. In the long run, too, the hold of the Chinese ties with Soviet Russia was open to question. In the immediate future, however, the United States seemed unable or unwilling to give up its essentially unilateral program of military intervention in the Far East.

In the era of the Cold War the state of American public opinion would not permit the United States to abandon Chiang Kai-shek and his Nationalist government. Under the leadership of Secretary of State John Foster Dulles the American people were carried to the brink of war over the protection of anti-Communist regimes in Taiwan and Indo-China, but on the whole there was diminishing support for the idea of massive wars of liberation on the continents of Asia or Europe. Despite Republican party campaign talk of seizing the offensive against communism in order to free the peoples of the satellite countries, there were growing signs in the mid-1950's of some relaxation in the Cold War. And, in 1953, the death of Stalin and President Eisenhower's inauguration paved the way for a reconsideration of the rigid foreign policies that had characterized both the Truman Administration and the Kremlin.

Despite the popular postwar image of American omnipotence in international affairs, the United States, no more than the Soviet Union, was all-powerful. Unrest and revolt in the satellite countries, plus the independent course charted by Tito in Yugoslavia and Mao in China, were indications that the Communist world and Communist policy could no longer be dictated to automatically by Moscow. At the same time the stirrings in Western Europe, and particularly the reassertion of French power and influence, forced American policy makers to be more aware of popular sentiment for peace and neutralism. There was also the vital question of how long West Germany would remain a creature of the United States, willing to accept the lead of NATO and of American foreign policy. Finally the growth of an uncommitted bloc of Asiatic and African states within the United Nations had a moderating influence in the Cold War policies of the United States and Russia. As a climax to these developments, President Eisenhower and the top leaders of Russia, Great Britain, and France came together in the first of the famous summit meetings. There, at Geneva in July, 1955, the Soviet statesmen applauded Eisenhower's pledge to the world that the United States would never take part in an aggressive war.

Some moderation in the Cold War was also suggested in 1957 by one of its leading intellectual craftsmen, George F. Kennan. In his Reith Lectures in Britain Kennan, speaking as a private citizen, had the temerity to advance the possibility of a political settlement in Europe. As a first step, he urged that Soviet and Western forces be pulled back to make possible a neutralized zone, including a united Germany, in the heart of the Continent. Accepting the fact that the Soviet idea of the word "peace" was not the same as the West's, Kennan added, however:

> But I see no reason for believing that there are not, even in Moscow's interpretation of this ambiguous word, elements more helpful to us all than the implications of the weapons race in which we are now caught up. And I refuse to believe that there is no way in which we could combine a search for these elements with the pursuit of a reasonable degree of military security in a world where absolute security has become an outmoded and dangerous dream.[12]

Kennan's program of an orderly disengagement with a nuclear free zone in Europe won considerable popular support in the West as well as the continued backing of Adam Rapacki, the Foreign Minister of Poland. It was now possible in Europe, as around most

[12] G. F. Kennan, *Russia, the Atom and the West* (New York, 1958), 93.

of the world, to draw a line which both sides in the Cold War for the most part respected. Thus the United States did not intervene to aid Hungary's fight for freedom, and Russia avoided carrying its exploitation of the troubles in the Middle East and the Congo to the point of a general war. Even in Cuba, where alone in Latin America a Communist government was established and maintained, the Russians backed down and withdrew their missiles.

Cold War and containment policies, symbolized in such American slogans as Negotiation from Strength, Peace through Power, and Massive Retaliation, had perhaps become self-defeating. Since World War II a diplomatic revolution had taken place. Old enemies —Germany and Japan—had become allies of the United States, while Russia, a former ally, was now along with Red China the chief foe of the West. More wars were not likely to help the search for a durable peace. Instead, the hard policies adhered to in foreign affairs by both Russia and the United States had resulted by the mid-1950's in such a high level of military preparedness that it was doubtful if either country could win a war in which nuclear weapons were involved. Only limited wars seemed feasible in an era in which Russia had substantially caught up with the United States in the race for mastery in nuclear weapons.

In August, 1953, less than a year after the United States had exploded the first hydrogen bomb at Eniwetok, the Soviets set off a similar device somewhere in Siberia. The more than four-year gap after 1945 between the Soviet and American detonation of their first atomic bombs had now been significantly narrowed. More important therefore than the welter of technical military arguments as to which side had supremacy in atomic arms and missiles was the fact that, in the proliferation of nuclear weapons, a balance and a surplus had been reached. Henceforth any major war would entail the possible destruction not only of civilization but even of most forms of life on the surface of the planet. This possibility became even stronger as other nations were able to trigger their first nuclear explosions—first the British, then the French, and finally in October, 1964, the Chinese. Meanwhile Russian scientific prowess was further indicated when in 1957 the Soviets were able to anticipate the United States by many months in launching their first intercontinental ballistic missile and their first earth satellite—the famous Sputnik.

The nuclear stalemate enforced by the late 1950's was part of the growing frustrations of the Cold War. As an uneasy world experienced a continual succession of military crises in all parts of the globe, United States diplomacy seemed to alternate between the cautious approach of President Eisenhower and the aggressive techniques of his Secretary of State John Foster Dulles. This same ambivalence was illustrated in the contrast between the general spirit of goodwill in Soviet-American relations, following Premier Khrushchev's first visit to the United States in September, 1959, and the ensuing collapse of the projected Summit Meeting between Eisenhower and Khrushchev in Paris eight months later. All hopes for the high-level conference were destroyed on the eve of the meeting by the revelation that an American U-2 reconnaisance plane had been shot down deep in Russian territory.

The U-2 episode of May, 1960, underscored the extraordinary power and influence over American foreign policy which was being exercised by "an invisible government" made up of the various secret services of the United States—notably the Central Intelligence Agency or C.I.A. A year later in the Bay of Pigs invasion of Cuba, the C.I.A. failed to repeat the success of some of its earlier covert operations in Latin America. But both these incidents were unpleasant reminders of the dangers of the Cold War to the traditional values of American democracy—including the belief in at least some measure of popular control over foreign affairs.

In the 1960's the old hopes and fears which had marked the Cold War in the previous decade continue to affect the course of American diplomacy. Although Europe, despite its divided status, has achieved a remarkable degree of stability and prosperity, Berlin remains a troubled area symbolized by the Communist wall erected between the East and West sectors of the city. In the Far East the civil war in Vietnam threatens to involve the United States in a major struggle against the forces of Chinese communism. And over the Latin American policy of the United States there is the shadow cast by the Castro Communist regime in Cuba. In general, the Kennedy Administration proposed no fundamental changes in American foreign policy in the Cold War. As before, United States diplomacy rested on a continuing confidence in the power and ability of American military strength and nuclear force to contain communism, whether in its Russian or its Chinese form. And, indeed, at first, in the crises over Cuba and the Berlin Wall in 1961, it seemed possible that the Cold War would suddenly become hot.

Despite its frequently inconsistent attempts to gain both peace and victory in the Cold War, as for example in American policy toward Vietnam, the Kennedy administration did make a strong effort to reverse almost two decades of continual tension between the United States and the Soviet Union. Most important in this regard was the long-proposed Test-Ban Treaty by which the United States and the Soviet Union agreed to prohibit further nuclear explosions, except in a limited way underground. Hopefully the Test-Ban Agreement could also serve in the future as a first step in a general program of world disarmament. And President Kennedy himself, before his assassination, was also able to further the cause of world peace in a series of notable statements climaxed by his commencement address at American University on June 10, 1963. Calling for a new American attitude toward the possibility of reaching an understanding with the Soviet Union, the President urged a relaxation of the hatred and conflicts of the Cold War. To that end he declared that henceforth "the United States does not propose to conduct nuclear tests in the atmosphere so long as other states do not do so. We will not be the first to resume." [13]

In full support of President Kennedy's plea for mitigating the bitter feelings engendered by the Cold War, Senator William Fulbright, chairman of the Senate Foreign Relations Committee, stated the case for a more flexible American foreign policy. Without going so far as his colleague Wayne Morse, who argued for the essential withdrawal of the United States forces in Vietnam, Senator Fulbright advocated a greater degree of accommodation in American policies toward the Soviet Union, Cuba, and Red China. Exploring the conflict in foreign policy between old myths and present realities, Fulbright questioned the reality of the master myth of the Cold War that every Communist state was a threat to the Free World. Thus a policy of encouraging limited agreements and trade with some of

[13] *Public Papers of the Presidents, John F. Kennedy, 1963* (Washington, 1964), 463–464.

the nations in the Communist bloc might well serve the interests of the United States and hopes of world peace. In any case, the Senator concluded:

> We must dare to think "unthinkable thoughts." We must learn to explore all of the options and possibilities that confront us in a complex and rapidly changing world. We must learn to welcome rather than fear the voices of dissent. . . .[14]

Twenty years after the close of the Second World War, the American people, together with most of mankind, still sought the means of achieving a lasting peace. In the midst of the continuing strife and conflicts of the Cold War, there was ever more evidence and complaint that the diplomacy of containment had become sterile and self-defeating. Fashioned originally in 1947 to place pressure on the Soviet Union, containment had resulted instead in increasing the demands put upon the American people. Convinced that freedom everywhere depended on the United States, American planners engaged in an often desperate policy of universal military intervention and of massive economic aid to the nations of the Free World. Frantically bolstering up governments which, all too frequently, did not enjoy the support of their own peoples, the United States was able to do little more than maintain a military status quo in the Cold War. As the world alternated between the uncertain states of an uneasy peace and limited wars, there was always the danger that some minor incident or brush war would touch off a dreaded nuclear holocaust.

Though the Kennedy and Johnson administrations followed, on the whole, the inflexible policies set by their predecessors in regard to Cuba, Germany, South Vietnam, and Red China, the search for peace has not been abandoned. Some of the spirit of goodwill in Soviet-American relations, which had been lost over the U-2 incident and the failure of the last Summit Meeting between Khrushchev and Eisenhower, gradually returned after the Test-Ban Treaty, even though American foreign policy, like that of the Soviets, was still committed to the goal of an eventual political or military victory. Certainly the world scene remains troubled and confused. Only the future can reveal the eventual outcome of the American Cold War diplomacy of containment. Meanwhile American foreign policy

[14] J. W. Fulbright, *Old Myths and New Realities* (New York, 1964), 45.

faces the task, described by President Kennedy, to "labor on—not toward a strategy of annihilation but toward a strategy of peace." [15] These words of the late President are a reminder that, if a Third World War is indeed to be avoided, it is probable that history will pay tribute to those farsighted statesmen who, in looking beyond their own national interests, have been able to think in terms of all mankind.

SELECTED REFERENCES

Carleton, William G. *The Revolution in American Foreign Policy: Its Global Range*. New York: Random House, 1963.

Crabb, Cecil V. *Bipartisan Foreign Policy: Myth or Reality?* Evanston, Ill.: Row Peterson, 1957.

Donelan, Michael. *The Ideas of American Foreign Policy*. London: Chapman and Hall, 1963.

Fleming, D. F. *The Cold War and Its Origins, 1917–1960*. 2 vols. Garden City, N.Y.: Doubleday, 1961.

Graebner, Norman A. *Cold War Diplomacy: American Foreign Policy, 1945–1960*. Princeton, N.J.: Van Nostrand, 1962.

Horowitz, David. *The Free World Colossus: A Critique of American Foreign Policy in the Cold War*. New York: Hill and Wang, 1965.

Kennan, George F. *Russia, the Atom and the West*. New York: Harper, 1958.

Kissinger, Henry A. *Nuclear Weapons and Foreign Policy*. New York: Harper, 1957.

Lens, Sidney. *The Futile Crusade: Anti-Communism as American Credo*. Chicago: Quadrangle, 1964.

Lukacs, John. *A History of the Cold War*. Garden City, N.Y.: Doubleday, 1962.

Mills, C. Wright. *The Power Elite*. New York: Oxford University Press, 1956.

Sapin, Burton M. and Richard C. Snyder. *The Role of the Military in American Foreign Policy*. Garden City, N.Y.: Doubleday, 1954.

Spanier, John W. *American Foreign Policy Since World War II*. New York: Praeger, 1960.

Wise, David and Thomas B. Ross. *The Invisible Government*. New York: Random House, 1964.

[15] *Public Papers of the Presidents, John F. Kennedy, 1963*, 464.

Index